# Money Mindset Mastery

Maxwell Ryder

Published by Limitless Horizons Ink, 2024.

While every precaution has been taken in the preparation of this book, the publisher assumes no responsibility for errors or omissions, or for damages resulting from the use of the information contained herein.

MONEY MINDSET MASTERY

**First edition. December 30, 2024.**

Copyright © 2024 Maxwell Ryder.

Written by Maxwell Ryder.

# Table of Contents

Money Mindset Mastery .................................................................. 1
Chapter 1: The Foundations of a Wealthy Mindset ................... 7
Chapter 2: Breaking Free from Financial Fear .......................... 13
Chapter 3: The Law of Attraction and Money .......................... 19
Chapter 4: Mastering the Psychology of Wealth ....................... 25
Chapter 5: From Lack to Abundance: Changing Your Financial Narrative ........................................................................................ 31
Chapter 6: Developing a Growth Mindset for Financial Success ............................................................................................ 37
Chapter 7: The Power of Positive Thinking in Wealth Building .. 43
Chapter 8: Overcoming Money Blocks and Unhealthy Habits ... 49
Chapter 9: Building a Wealthy Mindset Through Gratitude ........ 55
Chapter 10: Creating a Vision for Your Financial Future ............. 61
Chapter 11: The Role of Discipline in Achieving Financial Goals ................................................................................................ 67
Chapter 12: Investing in Yourself: The Best Path to Wealth ......... 73
Chapter 13: Creating Multiple Streams of Income ....................... 79
Chapter 14: Money Management: Practical Strategies for Wealth Building ............................................................................................ 85
Chapter 15: Overcoming Debt and Building Credit ..................... 91
Chapter 16: Wealth Building through Smart Investing ................ 99
Chapter 17: The Role of Networking and Relationships in Financial Success ........................................................................... 105
Chapter 18: Managing Setbacks and Staying Focused on Your Financial Goals .............................................................................. 111
Chapter 19: Living a Life of Abundance: Beyond Money .......... 117
Chapter 20: Creating Your Own Path to Financial Freedom .... 123

# Introduction: Understanding the Power of Money Mindset

In the pursuit of wealth and success, there is a truth that often goes unnoticed: the most powerful tool at your disposal is not a special investment strategy, a lucrative job, or even a groundbreaking business idea. The most powerful tool you have is your mind.

Money, like any other aspect of life, is not simply a matter of external circumstances. While your income, career, and opportunities are certainly important, the way you think about money will determine your ability to attract it, manage it, and grow it. Your mindset shapes everything you do, and it can either propel you toward financial success or hold you back from achieving your full potential.

**What is Money Mindset?**

Money mindset refers to the beliefs, attitudes, and behaviors that you hold about money. It is the lens through which you view the world of finances. Your money mindset has been shaped by a variety of factors: your upbringing, cultural influences, personal experiences, and even the messages you received about money from the media, society, or family. These beliefs influence how you make decisions, how you handle challenges, and even how you feel about your own ability to create wealth.

For some, money mindset is based on the belief that money is scarce and hard to come by. These individuals may feel that no matter how hard they work, they will never be able to break free from financial struggle. On the other hand, others may have an abundance mindset, believing that there are limitless opportunities to generate wealth. They may approach challenges with a sense of possibility and confidence, trusting that they have the skills and knowledge to overcome obstacles.

**Why Mindset is the Key to Unlocking Financial Success**

The idea that mindset plays a crucial role in achieving financial success is not new. In fact, it has been a core principle of successful individuals for centuries. Whether you look at the lives of the wealthiest entrepreneurs, renowned investors, or individuals who have achieved financial freedom, a common thread ties them together: they all have a mindset focused on abundance, growth, and opportunity.

Think of it this way: if you want to become a successful investor, you need to think like an investor. If you want to achieve financial freedom, you need to develop the mindset of someone who already has financial freedom. The way you think about money dictates the decisions you make—whether you are budgeting, saving, investing, or pursuing new income opportunities.

The power of mindset is rooted in the concept of self-fulfilling prophecies. When you believe that you are capable of achieving wealth, you are more likely to take the actions necessary to make that belief a reality. However, when you hold limiting beliefs about money, you may unknowingly sabotage your own efforts to build wealth. This is why developing a positive, empowering money mindset is the first and most important step on your path to financial success.

**The Role of Limiting Beliefs in Shaping Your Financial Reality**

One of the most significant barriers to financial success is the presence of limiting beliefs about money. These are the deep-seated thoughts and convictions that shape how you view wealth and your own ability to attain it. Limiting beliefs often develop early in life, typically through the influence of family, culture, or past experiences. They can take many forms:

- "Money is the root of all evil."
- "I will never be rich because I come from a poor background."
- "I'm just not good with money."
- "I'll never be able to save or invest."
- "There's never enough money to go around."

These beliefs hold us back by reinforcing the idea that money is either out of our reach or that we don't deserve it. But here's the truth: limiting beliefs are not facts—they are just thoughts that we have accepted as truth. The moment you recognize that these beliefs are holding you back, you can start to challenge them and replace them with more empowering thoughts and beliefs that will propel you toward financial success.

The shift from a scarcity mindset to an abundance mindset is the foundation of financial transformation. An abundance mindset is the belief that there is more than enough money and opportunity in the world for everyone. When you believe that wealth is abundant and that you are worthy of it, you open the door to new possibilities and opportunities that were previously invisible.

**The Importance of Shifting Your Focus from Scarcity to Abundance**

One of the most profound shifts you can make in your money mindset is transitioning from a scarcity mindset to an abundance mindset. A scarcity mindset is rooted in the belief that resources are limited, and that there is never enough to go around. People with a scarcity mindset often experience feelings of fear, stress, and anxiety about money. They may hoard their resources, hesitate to invest in themselves or their future, and even avoid taking financial risks out of fear of losing what little they have.

On the other hand, an abundance mindset recognizes that there is no limit to what you can achieve or create. It is based on the belief that opportunities are endless, and that with the right knowledge, determination, and effort, anyone can build wealth. This shift in thinking opens up new avenues for success, whether it's through investing, starting a business, or simply becoming more financially responsible.

**The Power of Positive Thinking in Building Wealth**

The law of attraction, popularized by books like *The Secret*, teaches us that what we focus on expands. When you focus on abundance, prosperity, and the belief that you can create wealth, you are more likely to attract those opportunities into your life. But this doesn't mean that wealth simply falls into your lap by thinking positively—it means that when you focus on abundance, you become more aware of opportunities that align with your financial goals.

By practicing positive thinking and affirming your belief in your ability to achieve wealth, you align your thoughts with the actions required to create financial success. This could mean taking small steps, like creating a budget, investing in your education, or seeking out new income streams. As you begin to take action based on a positive, growth-oriented mindset, you will start to see results.

**Taking Responsibility for Your Financial Journey**

Another crucial aspect of money mindset is taking full responsibility for your financial journey. Many people fall into the trap of blaming external factors for their financial struggles—whether it's the economy, their upbringing, or bad luck. While external factors do play a role, the truth is that you have the power to control your financial destiny.

Taking responsibility means recognizing that your financial future is in your hands. No one else can determine how much wealth you create except for you. This sense of ownership is incredibly empowering, and it opens the door for you to take the necessary actions to transform your financial situation.

**Setting the Stage for Financial Mastery**

In this book, we will explore the key principles and strategies that will help you unlock the path to wealth and abundance. You will learn how to:

- Develop a mindset that attracts wealth and opportunities.
- Overcome limiting beliefs and money blocks.
- Cultivate healthy financial habits.
- Build multiple streams of income.
- Invest in your personal growth and development.
- Manage and grow your wealth for long-term financial freedom.

# MONEY MINDSET MASTERY

This journey will require dedication and commitment, but with the right mindset, you can achieve financial freedom and abundance. The tools and strategies you'll learn in the following chapters will help you transform your relationship with money, develop the habits of wealthy individuals, and ultimately build the life you desire.

Are you ready to take control of your financial destiny and unlock the path to wealth? Your journey to mastering your money mindset begins now

# Chapter 1: The Foundations of a Wealthy Mindset

We live in a world where wealth is often seen as the ultimate symbol of success. From the towering skyscrapers in major cities to the luxurious cars on the streets, money and the things it can buy have become synonymous with achievement, status, and happiness. But what if I told you that wealth isn't just about the amount of money you have in your bank account or the possessions you own? What if the secret to unlocking true financial freedom is not found in the external world, but in the way you think?

A wealthy mindset is the foundation of lasting success. Without the right mindset, no amount of money or external success will ever be enough. You may reach your financial goals, but without the proper mental framework, you'll likely find yourself feeling unfulfilled, stressed, or even worse, stuck in a cycle of financial struggle, despite your best efforts. So, how do you cultivate a wealthy mindset? How do you move beyond the limitations of conventional thinking and truly begin to unlock your potential to create and grow wealth?

In this chapter, we will lay the groundwork for developing a wealthy mindset. We will explore the core principles that drive wealth creation, and how to reshape your thoughts and beliefs about money. By the end of this chapter, you'll have the tools and insights needed to begin shifting your mindset toward one that attracts prosperity, abundance, and lasting financial freedom.

**The Role of Money Mindset in Financial Success**

When we talk about money mindset, we're not just referring to how much you value money, but rather how you think about and approach it. Money mindset encompasses everything from your beliefs about earning, saving, spending, investing, and giving, to the attitudes you have toward financial challenges and setbacks.

Wealthy people don't just think differently about money; they think differently about their ability to earn and manage it. They view money as a tool for freedom, growth, and opportunity. They see challenges not as obstacles, but as stepping stones to greater success. Their mindset is rooted in abundance, not scarcity.

The first step toward developing a wealthy mindset is understanding how much your current thoughts and beliefs about money influence your financial reality. If you have limiting beliefs or a negative relationship with money, those thoughts will guide your actions and ultimately shape the results you get. For example, if you believe that money is hard to come by, you may hesitate to invest in opportunities that could grow your wealth. If you believe that wealthy people are greedy or selfish, you may subconsciously avoid wealth-building activities because you don't want to adopt those traits.

Conversely, if you adopt a mindset of abundance and opportunity, you'll start to see money as a tool to create more freedom and choice in your life. You'll begin to attract opportunities, make wiser financial decisions, and embrace challenges with the belief that you have the power to overcome them.

**Shifting from Scarcity to Abundance Thinking**

One of the key principles of a wealthy mindset is the shift from scarcity thinking to abundance thinking. Scarcity thinking stems from the belief that resources—whether money, time, or opportunity—are limited. When you view the world through the lens of scarcity, you believe that if someone else has something, it means less for you. Scarcity thinking creates feelings of fear, competition, and stress, and it leads to behaviors that are focused on hoarding, protecting, and avoiding risk.

On the other hand, abundance thinking operates under the belief that there is more than enough for everyone. It's the understanding that opportunities are endless, resources are abundant, and wealth is not a finite pie that gets divided up but an expansive ecosystem that grows the more we invest in it.

When you shift to an abundance mindset, your outlook on money—and life in general—changes dramatically. You no longer view others' success as a threat to your own. You begin to see opportunities where others see barriers. You feel confident taking calculated risks and know that even if you fail, there are countless other opportunities ahead of you.

Shifting from scarcity to abundance requires a conscious effort. It requires letting go of old, limiting beliefs and replacing them with new, empowering ones. It's about rewiring your brain to focus on the possibilities rather than the limitations.

**The Power of Beliefs: Rewriting Your Money Story**

Our beliefs about money are often shaped by early experiences. From a young age, we absorb messages about money from our parents, teachers, peers, and the media. These messages form the foundation of our money story—the narrative we tell ourselves about money. Our money story influences everything from how we spend and save, to how we feel about our ability to achieve financial success.

Take a moment to reflect on your own money story. What messages did you receive about money growing up? Did your parents struggle with money? Were you taught that money doesn't grow on trees, or were you encouraged to dream big and aim for financial success?

It's important to recognize that your money story is not set in stone. It can be rewritten at any time. The beliefs that once held you back from achieving financial success can be replaced with new, empowering beliefs that allow you to step into your full financial potential.

To start rewriting your money story, you need to identify the limiting beliefs that have been holding you back. Here are a few common ones:

- **"Money is hard to come by."** This belief often stems from early experiences of financial struggle, and it can create a sense of resistance toward wealth-building activities.
- **"I'm not good with money."** This belief can prevent you from taking control of your finances or seeking out new ways to improve your financial situation.
- **"Money is the root of all evil."** This belief is often influenced by societal or religious teachings and can create guilt around the pursuit of wealth.

Once you've identified your limiting beliefs, challenge them. Ask yourself whether they are truly true, or if they are simply stories you've been telling yourself. Replace them with empowering beliefs that support your vision of wealth and abundance. For example:

- **"Money flows easily and abundantly into my life."**
- **"I am capable of managing and growing my money."**
- **"Wealth is a tool for freedom, growth, and contribution."**

**Embracing the Growth Mindset for Wealth Creation**

A growth mindset, popularized by psychologist Carol Dweck, is the belief that your abilities and intelligence can be developed through hard work, dedication, and learning. People with a growth mindset see challenges as opportunities to grow and improve. They don't shy away from failure; instead, they see it as a necessary step toward mastering a skill or achieving success.

When it comes to building wealth, adopting a growth mindset is essential. Wealth creation is not about finding a quick fix or relying on luck. It's about continuously improving, learning new skills, and adapting to changing circumstances.

To cultivate a growth mindset, focus on the process of learning rather than the outcome. Take pleasure in the journey of financial education and self-improvement. Whether you're learning about investing, money management, or entrepreneurship, approach each new challenge with curiosity and enthusiasm. Embrace the idea that every setback is an opportunity to learn and grow.

### The Importance of Patience and Consistency

Building wealth is a long-term endeavor. It doesn't happen overnight. A common mistake people make is expecting quick results, and when they don't see immediate success, they give up. The reality is that creating lasting financial success requires patience, consistency, and a willingness to play the long game.

The key to wealth-building is consistency. Whether you're saving, investing, or growing your business, the more consistently you take action, the more likely you are to achieve your financial goals. Small, consistent steps will compound over time and lead to significant results.

### Creating a Wealthy Mindset in Practice

Now that you have an understanding of the foundational principles of a wealthy mindset, it's time to put them into practice. Here are some actionable steps you can take to begin developing your wealthy mindset:

1. **Start with gratitude.** Practice daily gratitude for the wealth you already have. Whether it's your health, relationships, or small financial wins, focusing on what you already have will shift your focus from scarcity to abundance.

2. **Affirm your belief in abundance.** Create a set of positive affirmations that align with your new beliefs about money. Say them out loud every day to reinforce your mindset.

3. **Educate yourself about money.** The more you know about finances, investing, and wealth-building strategies, the more confident and capable you'll feel. Read books, listen to podcasts, and seek out mentors who can guide you on your financial journey.

4. **Take action.** Mindset is important, but it's nothing without action. Start taking small steps toward your financial goals—whether it's creating a budget, setting up a savings plan, or investing in your education.

5. **Surround yourself with like-minded individuals.** The people you spend time with influence your mindset. Surround yourself with people who have a positive relationship with money and who inspire you to grow and succeed.

## Conclusion

Developing a wealthy mindset is the first step toward creating lasting financial success. It requires a shift in how you think about money, a willingness to let go of limiting beliefs, and a commitment to embracing the opportunities that come your way. As you begin to apply the principles of a wealthy mindset, you'll start to see shifts in your financial reality—more opportunities, greater abundance, and the confidence to take bold actions toward your goals.

Remember, the journey to wealth starts in the mind. When you change the way you think about money, you change the way you interact with the world, and you unlock the door to limitless possibilities.

# Chapter 2: Breaking Free from Financial Fear

Money often holds a strange power over us. Whether we're making decisions about how to spend, save, or invest, many of us are paralyzed by a deep-seated fear that prevents us from making the best choices for our financial futures. This fear is something that most of us can relate to, as it comes from a place of uncertainty, lack, or previous negative experiences. But the truth is, financial fear isn't something we have to live with. In this chapter, we will explore how to break free from this fear, replace it with a sense of empowerment, and step into the financial freedom that is within our reach.

**Overcoming Fear and Anxiety About Money**

It's no secret that money can cause stress. The fear of not having enough, the anxiety of making the wrong financial decision, or the panic of not being able to provide for our families are all common emotions tied to money. For many, the topic of money is one of the most stressful parts of daily life. We're taught from a young age to be afraid of debt, to fear the unknown, and to worry about whether we'll ever have enough to retire or live comfortably.

This anxiety often stems from one key belief: **money is scarce**. If we don't have enough now, we might never have enough. If we make one wrong move, everything could collapse. These are beliefs that are ingrained in us through upbringing, media portrayals of financial failure, and even the societal pressure of living up to a certain standard.

But what if we told you that fear, in its most basic form, is a natural emotion? It's our body's way of alerting us to potential danger. The problem arises when this fear is amplified and holds us back from taking proactive, informed steps toward improving our financial health.

**1. Acknowledge the Fear**

The first step in overcoming any fear is to acknowledge it. For many people, financial fear can be so overwhelming that it's hard to even think about taking steps to improve their situation. You may find yourself avoiding looking at your bank balance, avoiding conversations about money, or even feeling ashamed of your current financial state. This avoidance, however, only prolongs the cycle of fear and helplessness.

To break free, you must confront your fear head-on. Take a moment to ask yourself: What exactly am I afraid of? Are you afraid of debt? Of losing your job? Of not being able to save enough for retirement? Acknowledging your fear is the first step in understanding it and taking control.

**2. Understand the Source of the Fear**

Once you acknowledge your fear, it's important to understand where it's coming from. Is it based on past experiences, like growing up in a household where money was always tight? Or is it more about societal pressure, constantly being bombarded by media messages telling you that you need more to be happy or successful?

In many cases, our fears about money are rooted in experiences we've had or narratives we've internalized. If you grew up with the belief that "money doesn't grow on trees," or "rich people are greedy," these beliefs can shape your financial decisions later in life, even if they're not entirely accurate. Fear often comes from a lack of understanding and knowledge. The more we know about money—how it works, how to manage it, and how to make it grow—the less fear we'll have about it.

**Replacing Fear with Empowerment**

# MONEY MINDSET MASTERY

Once you've acknowledged and understood your fear, the next step is to replace it with empowerment. Fear is a paralyzing force, while empowerment is a driving force. Empowerment is about taking control of your financial future, making decisions based on knowledge and confidence, and believing that you can overcome obstacles and thrive.

**1. Focus on What You Can Control**

It's easy to feel helpless when it comes to money, especially when there are so many things out of our control. The economy, rising costs, and unexpected expenses can all feel overwhelming. However, one of the keys to overcoming financial fear is to focus on what you **can** control.

You may not be able to control the market, but you can control your spending habits. You may not be able to predict unexpected financial setbacks, but you can prepare for them with an emergency fund. The more you focus on what's within your control, the more empowered you'll feel.

**2. Educate Yourself**

Knowledge is one of the greatest tools for overcoming fear. Financial education doesn't have to be complicated or overwhelming. Start by learning the basics—how to budget, how to save, how to invest, and how to build credit. The more you understand about managing money, the less fear you'll have about making financial decisions.

Many people are afraid of investing simply because they don't know where to start. But you don't need to be an expert to begin investing. Start small, read books or listen to podcasts on the topic, and learn from others who have succeeded in building wealth. The more informed you are, the more confident you'll become in your ability to make wise financial choices.

**3. Take Small, Calculated Steps**

Empowerment comes from action. One of the most effective ways to overcome fear is to take small, manageable steps toward your financial goals. If you're in debt, take the first step by creating a debt repayment plan. If you don't have an emergency fund, start by saving a small amount each month. If you're afraid of investing, begin with a low-risk investment or a retirement fund.

Taking small steps helps build momentum. Each time you take action, you're proving to yourself that you're capable of handling your finances and that you have control over your financial future. This empowers you to take bigger steps as you gain confidence.

### 4. Reframe Your Thoughts Around Money

Another powerful way to replace fear with empowerment is by reframing your thoughts about money. Instead of viewing money as a source of anxiety, begin to see it as a tool—something that can help you achieve your goals, provide for your family, and create the life you want. Rather than seeing financial setbacks as failures, view them as opportunities to learn and grow.

Instead of thinking, "I'll never get out of debt," reframe that thought to, "I am taking the necessary steps to become debt-free." Instead of saying, "I'm not good with money," replace it with, "I am learning how to manage my finances better every day." These reframes create a more positive relationship with money, which in turn helps you feel more in control.

### Real-Life Stories of Overcoming Financial Struggles

Nothing helps to inspire change more than real-life stories of individuals who have faced financial fear and successfully overcome it. Here are three stories of people who went from financial fear to financial freedom:

### 1. Sarah's Story: From Debt to Financial Freedom

Sarah had always struggled with money. She grew up in a household where debt was a constant stress, and she carried that fear into adulthood. In her twenties, Sarah accumulated significant credit card debt, which only deepened her anxiety. Every month, she'd make minimum payments, but the balance never seemed to shrink. She was living paycheck to paycheck, terrified of what would happen if something unexpected came up.

But one day, she decided that enough was enough. Sarah educated herself on personal finance, created a budget, and developed a plan to pay off her debt. It took time, but with consistent effort and small sacrifices, she paid off all of her credit cards. Now, she has an emergency fund, an investment plan, and a healthy credit score. Sarah's story is proof that even when financial fear feels overwhelming, with knowledge and action, you can take control of your money and build a future of financial freedom.

**2. Marcus's Story: Overcoming the Fear of Investing**

Marcus had always been terrified of investing. He grew up hearing stories of people losing their life savings in the stock market, and the thought of risking his hard-earned money filled him with dread. For years, Marcus avoided investing, even though he knew it was important for his long-term financial health.

But after learning more about the stock market and understanding how investing works, Marcus took the plunge. He started by investing small amounts in low-risk mutual funds. Over time, his confidence grew, and he began investing in individual stocks. Today, Marcus has a diversified portfolio and feels empowered about his financial future. He's realized that fear of investing was holding him back from reaching his full potential.

**3. Maria's Story: Transforming a Scarcity Mindset**

Maria grew up with a scarcity mindset. She was taught that money was hard to come by and that she had to work tirelessly to get by. As an adult, Maria found herself constantly stressing about money. No matter how much she earned, it never seemed like enough. She lived paycheck to paycheck, always afraid that something would go wrong.

One day, Maria realized that her fear wasn't coming from her circumstances but from her mindset. She began to reframe her thoughts about money and adopted an abundance mindset. She learned to manage her spending, started saving, and eventually began investing. Maria's financial situation changed dramatically, and she's now living the life she always wanted, free from the anxiety that once controlled her.

## CONCLUSION

Fear of money is a common experience, but it doesn't have to control your life. By acknowledging your fear, educating yourself, taking small steps, and reframing your thoughts, you can transform your financial anxiety into empowerment. When you replace fear with knowledge and action, you unlock the power to make smart financial decisions, attract opportunities, and build a future of wealth and freedom. The key to breaking free from financial fear is understanding that you have the power to change your mindset and take control of your financial destiny.

# Chapter 3: The Law of Attraction and Money

The concept of the **Law of Attraction** has gained significant attention in recent years, particularly in relation to manifesting wealth and abundance. While it may seem like a mystical or abstract idea to some, the Law of Attraction is based on a simple principle: like attracts like. This means that the thoughts, beliefs, and energy you project into the world will attract similar energy back to you. In this chapter, we will explore how the Law of Attraction influences wealth creation, practical steps to manifest financial abundance, and how to align your thoughts with your financial goals.

**How the Law of Attraction Influences Wealth Creation**

At its core, the Law of Attraction is rooted in the idea that **thoughts create reality**. What you focus on expands, and the energy you put out into the universe will return to you in ways that align with that energy. This can be incredibly powerful when it comes to attracting wealth and abundance into your life. However, it's not just about wishing for money or hoping it will fall into your lap. It's about cultivating the right mindset, beliefs, and actions that will draw financial prosperity to you.

**1. The Power of Positive Thinking**

One of the fundamental principles of the Law of Attraction is the idea that positive thoughts lead to positive outcomes. When it comes to money, this means that if you have a mindset of abundance, you are more likely to attract opportunities for wealth. Conversely, if you constantly worry about not having enough money or fear financial scarcity, that is what you are likely to manifest in your life.

The Law of Attraction operates on the premise that the universe responds to your vibrational frequency. Your thoughts, feelings, and emotions send out signals to the universe, and those signals attract similar energy. So, if you focus on thoughts of prosperity, financial freedom, and abundance, you are signaling to the universe that you are ready to receive wealth.

### 2. Visualization and Belief

Visualization is a powerful tool in manifesting wealth through the Law of Attraction. When you visualize yourself already having the wealth you desire—whether it's in the form of a dream home, a thriving business, or a large bank balance—you are sending a clear message to your subconscious mind that this reality is possible. The more you visualize your financial goals as already achieved, the more you program your mind to believe that wealth is not only possible but inevitable.

Belief is another key element. The Law of Attraction requires you to **believe** that what you want is already on its way to you. Doubts and negative beliefs about money can block the flow of abundance. If you don't believe you deserve wealth or feel that money is inherently difficult to come by, you are likely to attract scarcity instead of prosperity. Changing these limiting beliefs is a crucial step in aligning your mindset with the financial abundance you want to manifest.

### 3. Gratitude and Wealth

Gratitude is one of the most powerful tools in the Law of Attraction. The more you express gratitude for the money you already have, the more the universe will bring you reasons to be grateful for additional wealth. Gratitude shifts your focus from lack to abundance, which helps you maintain a positive mindset and attract more opportunities for financial growth.

When you show appreciation for the money you already possess, whether it's a paycheck, an unexpected gift, or savings in your account, you send a message to the universe that you are ready and willing to receive more. Gratitude is the energy that amplifies your wealth frequency and accelerates the manifestation process.

**Practical Steps to Manifest Financial Abundance**

Now that we understand the basic principles of the Law of Attraction, let's dive into the practical steps you can take to manifest financial abundance in your life.

**1. Clarify Your Financial Goals**

Before you can begin manifesting wealth, it's important to have a clear vision of what you want. The more specific your financial goals are, the easier it will be for you to focus your energy and intentions on them. Take some time to think about what financial abundance looks like for you. Do you want to pay off debt? Save for retirement? Start a business? Buy a house?

Once you have your goals in mind, write them down. Writing your goals solidifies them in your mind and creates a roadmap for your manifestation. Be specific about the amount of money you want to manifest, the timeline in which you want to achieve it, and the exact steps you are willing to take to reach those goals.

**2. Practice Daily Visualization**

Visualization is one of the most effective tools in the Law of Attraction, and it can be particularly powerful when it comes to manifesting money. Set aside time every day to visualize your financial goals as already achieved. Imagine yourself living in the home you've always wanted, traveling the world, or running a successful business. Feel the emotions that come with these accomplishments—joy, freedom, excitement.

The more vivid and real your visualization, the more it will influence your subconscious mind. Remember to **emotionally connect** with your visualization. The stronger the emotions you attach to your vision, the more likely you are to attract it into your life.

**3. Affirmations for Abundance**

Affirmations are another tool that can help align your thoughts with your financial goals. By repeating positive statements about money, you begin to reprogram your subconscious mind and break free from limiting beliefs about wealth. Some examples of powerful money affirmations include:
- "I am worthy of financial abundance."
- "Money flows to me easily and effortlessly."
- "I am open and receptive to all the wealth life offers me."
- "I am financially free and secure."
- "I attract opportunities to create wealth."

You can say these affirmations out loud or write them down every day. The more you repeat them, the more they will shape your mindset and create the financial abundance you desire.

### 4. Take Inspired Action

While the Law of Attraction focuses on the power of your thoughts, it's essential to pair this with inspired action. Manifestation isn't just about wishing for wealth to fall into your lap—it's about aligning your actions with your goals. If you want to attract financial abundance, take steps that move you closer to that goal.

This might mean taking a course to improve your skills, networking with like-minded individuals, creating a business plan, or cutting back on unnecessary expenses. Listen to your intuition and take action on the opportunities that arise. Trust that when you are aligned with your goals and the energy of abundance, the right opportunities will come to you.

### 5. Practice Gratitude for What You Have

As mentioned earlier, gratitude is a vital part of the Law of Attraction. Every day, take time to express gratitude for the money you already have. Whether it's the paycheck you receive, the financial support of loved ones, or even the small amount of money in your savings account, appreciating what you have sends a message to the universe that you are ready for more.

When you focus on gratitude, you shift your energy from lack to abundance, which helps to attract more wealth. Make a habit of writing down three things you're grateful for each day. Over time, this simple practice will help you cultivate a mindset of abundance that will support your financial goals.

### 6. Trust the Process

Manifestation requires patience and trust. When you set your intentions and take aligned action, trust that the universe will bring your desires to you in the right time and in the right way. Let go of the need to control how or when wealth will come to you. Have faith that it's already on its way.

Trusting the process means that even when things seem slow or difficult, you maintain your belief that your financial abundance is inevitable. The Law of Attraction works in mysterious ways, and sometimes the universe has a plan that's even better than what you could have imagined.

### Aligning Your Thoughts with Your Financial Goals

The most important part of using the Law of Attraction to manifest wealth is to ensure that your thoughts are aligned with your financial goals. If you want to attract abundance, you need to think abundantly. This means letting go of limiting beliefs, focusing on your strengths, and staying positive in the face of challenges.

### 1. Let Go of Limiting Beliefs

Many people unknowingly hold limiting beliefs about money, such as "money is the root of all evil," "I'll never be rich," or "I don't deserve financial success." These beliefs act as barriers to wealth creation and keep you trapped in a cycle of scarcity. To align your thoughts with your financial goals, you must identify and release these limiting beliefs.

Start by questioning the beliefs you have about money. Are they truly yours, or were they inherited from others? Are they based on fact or fear? Replace negative beliefs with empowering ones that support your wealth-building goals.

**2. Cultivate a Positive Money Mindset**

A positive money mindset is essential for manifesting wealth. Instead of focusing on what you don't have, focus on what you do have and how you can make the most of it. Practice abundance thinking by reminding yourself that money is not limited, and there is always enough to go around. Money is simply a tool that can be used to create the life you desire.

**Conclusion**

The Law of Attraction is a powerful tool for manifesting financial abundance. By aligning your thoughts, beliefs, and actions with your financial goals, you can attract the wealth and opportunities you desire. Remember, the process takes time, but with consistent effort, positive thinking, and inspired action, you will begin to see your financial reality shift. When you embrace the Law of Attraction, you not only change your mindset but also open yourself to the limitless potential of creating the wealth and freedom you deserve.

# Chapter 4: Mastering the Psychology of Wealth

Money is not just a physical resource; it is deeply intertwined with psychology. The way we think about money, the beliefs we hold about it, and the emotions it triggers play a crucial role in determining our financial success. This chapter explores the psychology of wealth, how to develop the mindset of the rich and successful, and the vital role self-worth plays in achieving financial prosperity.

**Understanding the Psychology of Wealth**

The psychology of wealth goes beyond just earning money—it involves the attitudes, behaviors, and thought processes that shape our relationship with money. Wealthy individuals don't necessarily have better financial opportunities than others, but they often possess a unique mindset that drives them to take action, stay disciplined, and maintain their financial goals despite obstacles.

**1. The Mindset of Abundance vs. Scarcity**

One of the most fundamental psychological distinctions between wealthy individuals and others is their mindset. **People with an abundance mindset** believe that there is more than enough wealth to go around and that they are deserving of their share. They see money as a tool to create opportunities, expand their possibilities, and enrich their lives and the lives of others.

In contrast, individuals with a **scarcity mindset** believe that money is limited and difficult to acquire. They may feel that no matter how hard they work, they will always struggle financially. This belief often leads to fear, anxiety, and hesitation when it comes to making money-related decisions.

The psychology of wealth teaches us that abundance is not just about having more money; it's about developing an outlook that sees possibility rather than limitation. By embracing an abundance mindset, you open yourself up to financial opportunities, and most importantly, you allow yourself to receive the wealth you deserve.

**2. The Role of Emotions in Wealth Building**

Our emotions play a powerful role in our financial lives. Fear, guilt, shame, and anxiety can create barriers that prevent us from achieving financial success. These emotions often stem from deep-seated beliefs about money that are ingrained over time.

For instance, many people carry **negative beliefs** such as "Money doesn't grow on trees," or "Rich people are greedy." These beliefs, even if unconscious, trigger emotional responses that keep them from taking action, taking risks, or pursuing opportunities that could lead to financial success.

On the other hand, emotions like **confidence, excitement, and gratitude** can propel us forward in our wealth-building journey. The psychology of wealth suggests that we need to **embrace positive emotions** around money—feeling empowered and open to receiving wealth, trusting that financial success is within our reach, and being comfortable with the idea of being financially prosperous.

**3. The Power of Self-Talk and Beliefs**

Your internal dialogue—the way you talk to yourself—greatly affects your financial outcomes. If your self-talk is filled with negative statements such as "I'll never be rich" or "Money is the root of all evil," these beliefs will shape your actions and reinforce limiting behaviors. To master the psychology of wealth, you must reframe your thinking.

Start by becoming aware of your negative self-talk about money and replace it with positive, empowering affirmations. For example, replace "I don't have enough money" with "I am capable of creating unlimited wealth." By consistently shifting your internal dialogue, you will reshape your beliefs and create new neural pathways that support financial abundance.

### Developing the Mindset of the Rich and Successful

The mindset of wealthy individuals is one of the most significant factors behind their financial success. This mindset is not just about having money, but it's about the **way they think, approach challenges, and make decisions.**

#### 1. Vision and Goals

Wealthy individuals have a clear vision of what they want and set specific, measurable goals to achieve their financial desires. This vision acts as a guiding force, helping them make strategic decisions and stay focused on their long-term objectives.

Successful individuals don't just make decisions based on short-term benefits. They consistently ask themselves, "Does this move me closer to my goal?" or "How will this affect my financial future?" They are always working toward a bigger picture, understanding that wealth accumulation is a process that requires both patience and effort.

By creating a clear financial vision and setting goals that are both specific and measurable, you align yourself with the same mindset that wealth builders use. **Create your vision**, write down your goals, and break them into actionable steps to ensure you're working toward something tangible.

#### 2. Delayed Gratification

One of the key traits of wealthy individuals is their ability to delay gratification. In a society that often values instant rewards, wealth builders understand that the pursuit of long-term goals requires sacrifices in the short-term.

This might mean forgoing unnecessary luxuries in order to invest in education, business ventures, or saving for future needs. Delaying gratification doesn't mean denying yourself the enjoyment of life—it means making conscious decisions to invest in your future self.

For example, instead of spending money on items that provide temporary pleasure, you might choose to invest in assets that generate long-term wealth, such as stocks, real estate, or education. The ability to resist short-term temptations and focus on future rewards is a hallmark of the psychology of wealth.

### 3. Taking Calculated Risks

Another essential aspect of the rich and successful mindset is the ability to take calculated risks. While many people shy away from risk out of fear or uncertainty, wealthy individuals understand that risk is an inherent part of success. They do not take reckless risks, but they are willing to step out of their comfort zone to pursue new opportunities.

The psychology of wealth encourages you to evaluate risks carefully, assess the potential rewards, and make decisions based on logic and reason, not emotion. Taking well-thought-out risks is often the difference between staying stuck in your current situation and achieving significant financial growth.

### 4. Continuous Learning and Growth

Successful individuals never stop learning. They understand that in order to stay ahead financially, they must continuously educate themselves, whether through formal education, mentorship, or self-study. The rich and successful mindset is one of **constant growth**—financial growth, personal development, and learning new skills.

This mindset involves seeking opportunities for improvement and never believing that you've "arrived." Whether it's learning about new investment strategies, improving your financial literacy, or learning how to manage your emotions better, wealth-building is a journey of growth.

You should also seek out mentorship or surround yourself with others who share your financial goals. **Learning from others** who have successfully built wealth can offer valuable insights and accelerate your journey toward financial prosperity.

# MONEY MINDSET MASTERY

### The Role of Self-Worth in Financial Success

Self-worth plays a pivotal role in achieving financial success. If you don't believe you are worthy of wealth, it becomes much harder to achieve it. **Your relationship with money is often a reflection of your relationship with yourself.** How you see yourself, your skills, and your value directly influences your ability to attract and manage money.

### 1. Believing You Deserve Wealth

One of the most significant obstacles people face in building wealth is the belief that they don't deserve it. This belief is often rooted in early life experiences, societal messages, or limiting beliefs about money. If you struggle with feelings of unworthiness, you may find yourself subconsciously sabotaging your financial success.

To overcome this, you need to **affirm your worthiness**. Recognize that you have unique talents, skills, and value to offer the world. Wealth is not reserved for a select few; it is available to everyone who is willing to embrace abundance and take steps toward their goals.

By developing a deep sense of self-worth, you not only believe that you deserve financial success, but you also open yourself to receiving it. **Trust in your value** and begin to take actions that align with your worth.

### 2. Letting Go of Money Shame

Another barrier to wealth is **money shame**—the belief that money is "bad" or that you are somehow morally wrong for wanting financial success. This shame can prevent you from seeking wealth and achieving the success you deserve.

To release money shame, it's important to **shift your perspective** on money. Money is simply a tool—a means to an end. It can be used for good or ill, but it is not inherently bad. Wealth can be a force for positive change when used wisely.

### Conclusion

Mastering the psychology of wealth is essential for building lasting financial success. By developing an abundance mindset, embracing positive emotions about money, and cultivating the mindset of the rich and successful, you can create the financial future you desire. The psychology of wealth isn't just about having money—it's about the way you think about, interact with, and make decisions regarding money. When you understand the role of self-worth and belief in financial success, you set yourself up for a prosperous future. The journey to wealth begins in the mind, and once you master the psychology of wealth, the financial results will follow.

# Chapter 5: From Lack to Abundance: Changing Your Financial Narrative

Money is more than just a tool—it is a reflection of our mindset, our beliefs, and, in many cases, our past experiences. The way we view money is shaped by the narrative we've constructed over time. Unfortunately, for many of us, this narrative is filled with limitations, negative beliefs, and a deep sense of lack. These beliefs are often deeply ingrained in our subconscious, formed from past experiences and societal conditioning.

However, just as any story can be rewritten, so can the narrative we hold about money. Changing your financial narrative is not simply about earning more money; it's about altering the way you view money, the opportunities you see, and the possibilities you believe are available to you. It is about shifting from a place of scarcity to one of abundance, from feeling stuck in a cycle of struggle to embracing a future filled with wealth and prosperity.

In this chapter, we will explore how to rewrite your money story, the profound impact of past experiences on your financial outlook, and how to transform negative beliefs into positive affirmations that can set you on a path to financial abundance.

**Rewriting Your Money Story**

We all have a money story—a narrative that we carry with us, often without even realizing it. This story is influenced by our childhood, our family's relationship with money, the culture we grew up in, and our own personal experiences. These influences shape our perceptions of money and how we feel about it.

For example, if you grew up in a family where money was scarce, you may have internalized the belief that there is never enough to go around. You may have witnessed your parents working hard, struggling to make ends meet, and perhaps even fighting about money. This creates a story in your mind that reinforces the idea of financial struggle, scarcity, and stress.

Conversely, if you grew up in an environment where wealth was abundant, your money story may revolve around ease, comfort, and the belief that money is always available when needed. You may have internalized the idea that wealth is something that comes naturally to you, and you may approach your finances with confidence and optimism.

These stories, however, are not fixed. They are narratives that we have written over time, and just like any good story, they can be edited, rewritten, and reframed to create a better ending.

To begin rewriting your money story, it's important to first **become aware of your current narrative**. Pay attention to the thoughts and beliefs you have about money. Do you think it's hard to make money? Do you believe that you will always struggle financially? Or do you view money as a tool for freedom and opportunity?

Once you identify your current narrative, ask yourself: **What beliefs or past experiences are influencing this story?** Are these beliefs truly yours, or were they passed down to you by others? **Are they serving you, or are they holding you back?**

Rewriting your money story requires courage and vulnerability. It involves confronting the limiting beliefs you hold about money and replacing them with empowering thoughts and perspectives. Start by **shifting your focus** from what you don't have to what you do have. Look at your current financial situation and identify areas of abundance, no matter how small. Even the ability to pay for basic needs is a form of abundance. From this place of gratitude, you can begin to envision a new financial story, one where wealth is abundant and opportunities are endless.

## The Impact of Past Experiences on Your Financial Outlook

Many of our beliefs about money are rooted in past experiences—experiences that we may have long since forgotten, yet they continue to shape our financial reality. These experiences could be rooted in childhood, our first jobs, relationships, or even societal messages we've internalized.

For example, you may have grown up hearing phrases like, "Money doesn't grow on trees" or "The rich get richer, and the poor get poorer." These phrases, although innocent at the time, can have a deep psychological impact, planting seeds of doubt and scarcity in your subconscious mind. As a result, you may find yourself struggling to make ends meet, even if you're putting in the hard work.

Or perhaps your first experience with money was one of loss—losing a job, going through bankruptcy, or facing financial hardships that made you feel powerless and vulnerable. These events can create a sense of **fear and anxiety around money**, causing you to avoid thinking about finances or to react impulsively when faced with financial decisions.

Another key influence on your financial outlook might be the financial behavior of your parents or caregivers. If they were constantly in debt, stressed about money, or made poor financial choices, you might have internalized these behaviors as normal. You may find yourself repeating the same patterns without even realizing it.

These past experiences have a profound impact on our money mindset. They form the lens through which we view financial opportunities, and they influence how we behave with money. However, acknowledging the influence of these experiences is the first step toward **reclaiming control** over your financial story.

To break free from the grip of your past experiences, it's important to **challenge the beliefs** that stem from them. Ask yourself: **Are these** beliefs still true for me today? Are they helping me grow and achieve my financial goals? Or are they keeping me stuck in a cycle of scarcity?

### Transforming Negative Beliefs into Positive Affirmations

One of the most powerful tools for changing your financial narrative is the use of positive affirmations. Affirmations are statements that **affirm your goals, desires, and positive beliefs**. They are designed to reprogram your subconscious mind and replace negative beliefs with empowering ones.

When it comes to money, most of us have negative beliefs that have been ingrained over years of experience. These beliefs might include:

- "I'll never be able to get out of debt."
- "Money is the root of all evil."
- "I'm not good with money."
- "There's never enough to go around."
- "Rich people are greedy."

These limiting beliefs create a mental block that prevents us from achieving financial success. However, the beauty of affirmations is that they **offer an alternative narrative**—one that empowers you to take control of your financial life.

To create positive affirmations that counter your negative beliefs, you need to identify what you truly want to believe about money. What would it look like if you truly embraced abundance? What would your life look like if you felt empowered and confident about your finances?

Start by writing down the negative beliefs that you hold about money. Then, for each negative belief, create a positive affirmation that challenges it. For example:

- Negative belief: "I'll never be able to get out of debt."
- Affirmation: "I am capable of paying off all my debts, and I am taking proactive steps toward financial freedom."
- Negative belief: "Money is the root of all evil."

- Affirmation: "Money is a tool that I use to create positive change and opportunities for myself and others."
- Negative belief: "I'm not good with money."
- Affirmation: "I am learning to manage my money wisely, and I am getting better every day."
- Negative belief: "There's never enough to go around."
- Affirmation: "I live in a world of abundance, and wealth is available to me at all times."
- Negative belief: "Rich people are greedy."
- Affirmation: "Wealth enables me to help others, contribute to my community, and create opportunities for those around me."

Once you have your affirmations, begin to **repeat them daily**. Say them aloud, write them down, and visualize yourself living out these affirmations. The more consistently you repeat them, the more they will begin to reprogram your subconscious mind.

Over time, you will start to notice a shift in your thoughts and behavior. You will feel more confident, more capable, and more empowered to take control of your finances. This transformation is not just about believing you can achieve financial success—it's about **embracing the belief that you are worthy** of that success, and that you have the power to make it happen.

### Conclusion

Changing your financial narrative is a powerful step toward financial freedom and abundance. By rewriting the story you've been telling yourself about money, you can transform your relationship with it and open up new possibilities for wealth and prosperity. Your past experiences may have shaped your financial outlook, but they do not define your future. You have the power to challenge limiting beliefs, rewrite your money story, and take positive steps toward financial success.

## MAXWELL RYDER

The journey from lack to abundance is one of personal growth, self-awareness, and empowerment. By shifting your mindset, embracing positive affirmations, and creating a new financial narrative, you can step into a future of unlimited wealth and opportunity. It's time to rewrite your story—because the life you deserve is waiting for you.

# Chapter 6: Developing a Growth Mindset for Financial Success

When it comes to achieving financial success, your mindset is perhaps the most powerful tool you possess. It shapes how you perceive opportunities, respond to challenges, and overcome setbacks. A growth mindset, as opposed to a fixed mindset, can make all the difference in your journey toward wealth and abundance.

A growth mindset is the belief that intelligence, abilities, and skills can be developed over time through hard work, perseverance, and learning. When it comes to money, this means understanding that financial success is not determined by your current circumstances, but by your ability to learn, adapt, and improve. With a growth mindset, you believe that you can always get better—whether it's managing your money, learning about investments, or developing new ways to generate wealth.

In this chapter, we will explore how to embrace continuous learning, overcome the fear of failure, and set and achieve money-related goals—three key components of developing a growth mindset for financial success.

**Embracing Continuous Learning**

One of the most defining features of a growth mindset is the commitment to continuous learning. In today's rapidly changing world, the most successful people are those who constantly seek new knowledge, skills, and strategies. When it comes to financial success, this is especially important. The world of money, investments, and personal finance is vast and constantly evolving. From stock market trends to new financial technologies, there's always something new to learn.

To develop a growth mindset for financial success, you need to embrace the idea that learning never stops. No matter where you are on your financial journey, there's always room to grow. This could mean educating yourself about basic financial principles like budgeting and saving, or diving deeper into more advanced topics like investing, real estate, or entrepreneurship.

The key to embracing continuous learning is to **remain curious** and open to new ideas. Here are some ways you can incorporate continuous learning into your financial life:

1. **Read Books and Articles**: There's a wealth of information available in books, blogs, and articles written by financial experts. Start by reading personal finance books that teach you the fundamentals of budgeting, saving, and investing. As you gain more confidence, expand your reading to include books on entrepreneurship, wealth creation, and advanced investment strategies.

2. **Listen to Podcasts and Watch Videos**: If you're short on time, podcasts and videos are a great way to learn on the go. There are countless podcasts that focus on personal finance, wealth-building, and mindset. Listening to these experts can provide valuable insights and motivate you to take action.

3. **Attend Workshops and Seminars**: Learning from experts in person or through online workshops can accelerate your financial education. Look for seminars or webinars on topics you want to explore, whether it's investing, budgeting, or entrepreneurship.

4. **Learn from Mentors**: Seek out mentors who have achieved the financial success you aspire to. Mentorship is an invaluable way to accelerate your learning and avoid costly mistakes. A mentor can provide guidance, share their experiences, and help you navigate challenges.

5. **Practice Financial Literacy**: Financial literacy is the foundation of wealth-building. It's crucial to understand key concepts such as budgeting, credit, debt, saving, and investing. Once you have a solid grasp of the basics, you can move on to more advanced topics, but never stop refreshing your knowledge.

**Overcoming the Fear of Failure**

One of the most significant barriers to financial success is the fear of failure. Many people are afraid to take risks or try new things because they fear losing money, making mistakes, or not succeeding. This fear can hold you back from seizing opportunities and trying new strategies to build wealth.

However, **failure is not the enemy—it is a stepping stone to success**. Every successful person has encountered failure at some point in their journey. The difference between those who succeed and those who don't is how they respond to failure. People with a growth mindset view failure as a learning experience rather than a permanent setback. They understand that failure is a natural part of the learning process and an opportunity for growth.

Here are some strategies for overcoming the fear of failure and using it to your advantage:

1. **Reframe Failure as Feedback**: Instead of seeing failure as something to be ashamed of, reframe it as **valuable feedback**. Each time something doesn't work out, ask yourself: "What did I learn from this experience?" and "How can I do better next time?" Every failure is a lesson in disguise, teaching you how to improve and grow.

2. **Start Small**: If you're afraid of taking big risks, start small. Take small steps toward your financial goals so that you can build confidence and experience along the way. Whether it's opening a savings account or making your first investment, small wins will build momentum and reduce the fear of failure.

3. **Accept Risk as Part of Growth**: Every financial decision involves some degree of risk. Whether you're investing in the stock market, starting a business, or pursuing a new career, there's always a chance that things won't go as planned. Instead of avoiding risk, learn to **embrace it** as a necessary part of growth. When you take calculated risks, you open yourself up to new opportunities and rewards.

4. **Visualize Success**: One of the most powerful tools for overcoming fear is visualization. Take time each day to visualize yourself achieving your financial goals. See yourself confidently making decisions, taking action, and creating the wealth you desire. This positive mental imagery can help diminish fear and replace it with the belief that success is not only possible but inevitable.

5. **Surround Yourself with Supportive People**: The people you surround yourself with can have a huge impact on your mindset. Surround yourself with individuals who encourage you to take risks and who view failure as a learning opportunity. Being part of a positive and supportive community will help you feel more confident in your ability to handle challenges.

### Setting and Achieving Money-Related Goals

One of the most powerful ways to foster a growth mindset and take control of your financial future is by setting clear, actionable goals. Goal-setting is essential because it provides direction, motivation, and accountability. Without goals, it's easy to drift aimlessly, reacting to situations instead of proactively creating the financial future you desire.

To set and achieve meaningful money-related goals, you need to make sure that your goals are **specific, measurable, achievable, relevant, and time-bound**—this is often referred to as the SMART goal framework.

1. **Be Specific**: A vague goal like "I want to be wealthy" is too broad and doesn't give you a clear direction. Instead, set specific goals, such as "I want to save $5,000 in the next 12 months" or "I want to pay off

$10,000 of credit card debt within the next year." The more specific you are, the easier it is to create a plan of action.

2. **Make It Measurable**: Your goals should be measurable so that you can track your progress. If your goal is to increase your income, how much would you like to increase it by? If you're aiming to save more money, how much do you want to save each month? Measuring your progress helps keep you motivated and focused.

3. **Ensure It's Achievable**: While it's important to set ambitious goals, they should also be realistic. Don't set yourself up for failure by setting unattainable goals. Start with goals that stretch you but are still achievable within your current circumstances. For example, if you're currently saving $200 per month, an achievable goal might be to increase that to $300 per month over the next few months.

4. **Make It Relevant**: Your financial goals should align with your overall vision for your life. What do you want your financial future to look like? Whether it's owning a home, retiring early, or building a legacy for your family, your goals should reflect what matters most to you.

5. **Set a Timeframe**: Goals without deadlines can easily be put off indefinitely. Set a clear timeframe for achieving your goals. Whether it's 6 months, 12 months, or 5 years, having a deadline helps you stay focused and accountable.

Once you've set your financial goals, break them down into smaller, actionable steps. Instead of focusing solely on the end result, focus on the actions you need to take to reach that result. This could mean automating your savings, setting up a budget, or investing in education to improve your financial skills.

### Conclusion

Developing a growth mindset for financial success is about embracing continuous learning, overcoming the fear of failure, and setting and achieving money-related goals. A growth mindset empowers you to view challenges as opportunities, setbacks as lessons, and failures as stepping stones on your journey to financial abundance.

By adopting a growth mindset, you'll start to see money not as something that controls you, but as a tool you can use to create the life you desire. As you continue to learn, take risks, and set meaningful goals, you'll find that your financial potential is limitless. With the right mindset, your journey to financial success is not only possible—it's inevitable.

# Chapter 7: The Power of Positive Thinking in Wealth Building

When we think about wealth and financial success, most people immediately focus on practical strategies like budgeting, investing, or starting a business. While these are crucial elements of wealth-building, there's another powerful force that often goes unnoticed—the force of **positive thinking**. Your thoughts, beliefs, and mindset play a foundational role in determining your financial outcomes.

This chapter explores the incredible power of positive thinking and how it can accelerate your journey to wealth. We'll examine how you can harness the power of positive thoughts, reprogram your subconscious mind for success, and incorporate daily habits that reinforce positive money thinking. Together, these practices will help you develop a mindset that is not only aligned with wealth but actively attracts it into your life.

**Harnessing the Power of Positive Thoughts**

Your thoughts are not just fleeting mental events—they are powerful forces that shape your reality. The way you think about money, success, and abundance directly impacts your financial results. Positive thinking isn't about naive optimism or ignoring the challenges of life; it's about consciously choosing thoughts that support your financial goals rather than sabotaging them.

Think of your mind as a garden. The thoughts you plant in it are the seeds, and the outcomes you experience are the fruits. If you plant seeds of fear, doubt, and negativity about money, you will likely experience financial struggle and hardship. On the other hand, if you plant seeds of positivity, abundance, and confidence, you're more likely to reap the rewards of financial success.

Positive thinking, especially when it comes to money, involves cultivating thoughts that are aligned with your goals and aspirations. It's about replacing the limiting beliefs that hold you back with empowering thoughts that propel you forward. Here's how you can harness the power of positive thinking for wealth building:

1. **Affirmations**: Repeating positive affirmations is one of the simplest yet most effective ways to shift your mindset. Affirmations are statements that you repeat regularly to reprogram your subconscious mind. Examples include: "I am worthy of financial abundance," "Money flows to me effortlessly," or "I am capable of achieving all my financial goals." By consistently affirming these beliefs, you begin to internalize them, making them a natural part of your thinking.

2. **Visualization**: Visualization is a powerful technique used by some of the most successful individuals in the world. It involves mentally picturing yourself achieving your financial goals. Imagine yourself living in your dream home, driving your dream car, or checking your bank account and seeing your financial goals realized. The more vividly you can imagine this, the more likely it is to manifest in your reality. Positive visualization creates a sense of belief and confidence that propels you to take actions toward your financial success.

3. **Gratitude**: One of the most effective ways to boost your positivity is by practicing gratitude. Focusing on the abundance that already exists in your life—whether it's the money you have, your job, your health, or your relationships—helps shift your mindset from scarcity to abundance. When you are grateful for what you have, you attract more of it. Financial abundance flows to those who appreciate it.

4. **Positive Self-Talk**: The internal dialogue you have with yourself plays a huge role in shaping your financial reality. If you constantly

tell yourself, "I'll never be rich," or "Money is hard to come by," you reinforce those beliefs. On the other hand, replacing negative self-talk with positive, empowering statements such as "I am financially abundant," or "I am worthy of success" helps to reprogram your mindset for success.

### Reprogramming Your Subconscious Mind for Success

The subconscious mind is like a powerful autopilot that drives most of your actions and decisions. It's responsible for everything from how you handle stress to how you make decisions about money. However, many of us have subconscious beliefs that limit our ability to create wealth. These beliefs often stem from childhood, societal conditioning, or past experiences, and they can prevent us from achieving financial success.

The good news is that your subconscious mind is **not fixed**—it can be reprogrammed. Just like you can change the software on your computer, you can change the way your mind operates. The key is to consciously feed your subconscious mind with positive, empowering thoughts and beliefs about money.

Here are some ways to reprogram your subconscious mind for financial success:

1. **Affirmations for Subconscious Reprogramming**: Just as you can use affirmations to reinforce positive thinking, you can also use them to directly influence your subconscious. Repeating affirmations that are specifically tailored to challenge your limiting beliefs about money is incredibly powerful. For example, if you've always believed that "money is hard to come by," replace it with, "Money comes easily and abundantly to me." Over time, your subconscious mind will start to accept this new truth.

2. **Meditation**: Meditation is a practice that helps you quiet your mind and connect with your deeper consciousness. Through meditation, you can become more aware of the subconscious beliefs

that are holding you back and gently replace them with new, empowering ones. During meditation, focus on visualizing your financial goals and reinforcing positive beliefs about money. This process helps to strengthen the connection between your conscious and subconscious minds, creating lasting change.

3. **Hypnosis**: Hypnosis is another powerful tool for reprogramming your subconscious mind. It involves entering a relaxed state and allowing yourself to be open to positive suggestions. Many people use hypnosis to overcome financial anxiety, dissolve limiting beliefs, and instill positive thoughts about money. You can find guided hypnosis sessions that are specifically focused on wealth-building and success.

4. **Self-Reflection**: Taking time to reflect on your past beliefs about money is a crucial step in reprogramming your subconscious mind. Consider the messages you received about money growing up. Were they positive or negative? Did you see your parents struggle with money, or did they model abundance? Understanding the origin of your financial beliefs helps you identify and change the ones that no longer serve you.

### Daily Habits to Reinforce Positive Money Thinking

Creating lasting change in your financial mindset requires consistent effort. It's not enough to simply think positively about money once in a while; you need to actively nurture and reinforce positive thinking on a daily basis. Habits are the key to making positive thinking a natural and integral part of your life.

Here are some daily habits you can implement to reinforce positive money thinking:

1. **Morning Mindset Ritual**: Start your day with a powerful mindset ritual that sets the tone for the rest of the day. This could include reading your affirmations, visualizing your financial goals, practicing gratitude, or meditating. The way you start your day

influences your mindset and actions, so make it a priority to begin each day on a positive note.

2. **Positive Money Journal**: Create a money journal where you write down your financial goals, affirmations, and reflections each day. Journaling helps reinforce positive thinking by making it tangible and actionable. Every day, write about the progress you've made, the positive financial experiences you've had, and the abundance you're attracting.

3. **Focus on Solutions, Not Problems**: Throughout the day, challenge yourself to focus on solutions rather than problems. If you encounter a financial setback or challenge, instead of dwelling on the negative aspects, ask yourself: "What can I learn from this? How can I turn this situation into an opportunity for growth?" This shift in focus empowers you to maintain a positive outlook, even in the face of adversity.

4. **Surround Yourself with Positivity**: The people you spend time with and the media you consume play a huge role in shaping your thoughts. Surround yourself with individuals who have a positive and empowering relationship with money. Read books, listen to podcasts, or watch videos that inspire and motivate you to think positively about your financial future.

5. **Celebrate Small Wins**: Even if your financial goals feel far off, take time to celebrate small wins along the way. Whether it's saving an extra $100 this month or paying off a small debt, celebrate every step forward. These celebrations reinforce positive thinking and remind you that you are making progress toward your ultimate goals.

### Conclusion

The power of positive thinking in wealth-building cannot be overstated. By consciously choosing to think positively about money, you begin to attract wealth and abundance into your life. Reprogramming your subconscious mind for success and establishing daily habits that reinforce positive money thinking will keep you aligned with your financial goals and open the door to new opportunities.

Remember, wealth starts in the mind. As you cultivate a positive mindset, you'll find that your actions, decisions, and results naturally shift toward success. By harnessing the power of positive thinking, you are not only building a healthy relationship with money—you're also creating a financial future filled with possibility and abundance.

# Chapter 8: Overcoming Money Blocks and Unhealthy Habits

When it comes to building wealth and achieving financial success, there are certain invisible barriers that many people face. These barriers often prevent individuals from reaching their full potential and experiencing the abundance they desire. These barriers, or **money blocks**, can be deeply ingrained and may stem from past experiences, limiting beliefs, or unhealthy financial habits. In many cases, these blocks and habits are subconscious, meaning they operate beneath the surface, influencing your financial decisions without you even realizing it.

In this chapter, we'll dive into understanding money blocks and unhealthy habits, how to identify them, and most importantly, how to break free from their hold. Overcoming these obstacles is a crucial step in unlocking your financial potential and creating the wealth and freedom you deserve.

**Identifying Common Money Blocks**

Money blocks are mental barriers that limit your ability to attract and manage wealth. These blocks can manifest in various forms, such as a fear of money, a lack of self-worth, or an unhealthy relationship with financial success. Identifying and acknowledging these blocks is the first step to overcoming them.

Here are some common money blocks that many people face:

**1. Fear of Success**

While most people think they fear failure, many are actually more afraid of success. This fear may arise from the belief that they don't deserve to be wealthy or that financial success will bring complications and stress. People with this block may self-sabotage or hesitate to pursue opportunities that would lead to financial success.

This fear is often rooted in past experiences or societal conditioning that equates wealth with negative traits, such as greed, selfishness, or corruption. They may also fear that success will alienate them from their family and friends or change their identity in ways they don't understand.

### 2. Fear of Failure

The fear of failure is another prevalent money block. It's the belief that no matter how hard you try, you will never succeed financially. This fear often stems from past financial mistakes or the conditioning that "money doesn't grow on trees" or "you have to work hard for every penny." People with this block may procrastinate or avoid taking action because they don't want to experience failure.

This fear can also be compounded by the belief that wealth is only attainable by a select few, which makes the prospect of achieving financial success feel impossible. The result is a reluctance to take risks, try new things, or pursue financial opportunities that could lead to success.

### 3. Lack of Self-Worth

Many people feel they are unworthy of financial abundance. This money block often stems from childhood experiences where an individual may have felt that they didn't deserve certain privileges or that their efforts were never enough. This belief can persist into adulthood and prevent individuals from seeking better-paying jobs, negotiating salaries, or pursuing opportunities for wealth creation.

Individuals with a lack of self-worth may also struggle with money because they believe they don't deserve to have it or feel guilty about wanting more. This guilt often leads to self-sabotage or the inability to manage and grow their wealth.

### 4. Scarcity Mindset

# MONEY MINDSET MASTERY

A scarcity mindset is the belief that there is never enough to go around—whether it's money, opportunities, or resources. People with this mindset are often focused on lack and fear losing what they have. They may hoard money, avoid spending on necessary things, or obsess over saving because they believe that if they don't act this way, they'll run out of money.

Scarcity thinking often leads to missed opportunities because it breeds hesitation and a reluctance to take risks. People with a scarcity mindset may also feel envious or resentful of others who are successful, believing that someone else's success takes away from their own potential.

**5. Guilt Around Money**

Guilt around money often occurs when individuals feel that wealth is morally wrong or that wanting money means they are greedy or selfish. This guilt can be deeply ingrained, often originating from religious or cultural teachings that emphasize modesty and humility. While it's important to avoid materialism, having money or striving for financial success is not inherently bad.

People who experience guilt around money often struggle to spend or invest it, even in ways that could improve their lives or support their goals. They may also shy away from asking for raises, negotiating better financial deals, or celebrating financial successes because they feel undeserving.

**Practical Exercises to Overcome Financial Obstacles**

Overcoming money blocks is not a one-time event; it's a continuous process of self-awareness and action. The following exercises can help you identify and break free from your money blocks, rewire your relationship with money, and create a mindset that supports wealth-building.

**1. Identify Your Money Stories**

Start by reflecting on your personal beliefs and experiences surrounding money. Ask yourself:

- What was my first memory of money?
- What did my parents or caregivers teach me about money?
- How do I feel when I think about financial success?
- Are there any recurring patterns or negative thoughts about money in my life?

By journaling your thoughts, you can identify money stories and beliefs that have shaped your financial behavior. Recognizing these stories is essential for challenging and changing them. Once you are aware of these limiting beliefs, you can replace them with empowering ones that align with your goals.

## 2. Reframe Negative Thoughts

The next step in overcoming money blocks is to reframe your negative thoughts about money. When you catch yourself thinking thoughts like "I'll never be able to save enough," or "Money is too hard to come by," stop and replace them with positive affirmations.

For example, you could replace "I'll never be able to save enough" with "I am capable of saving and growing my wealth, one step at a time." Repeating these affirmations will help reprogram your subconscious mind and reinforce new, healthier beliefs about money.

## 3. Visualize Financial Abundance

Visualization is a powerful tool for overcoming money blocks. Take time each day to visualize yourself living the financial life you desire. Picture yourself living in your dream home, driving your ideal car, or achieving your financial goals. Feel the emotions associated with this success—joy, pride, security, and excitement.

Visualization helps to rewire your brain and create a positive association with money. By repeatedly visualizing financial success, you begin to reprogram your subconscious mind to accept this reality.

## 4. Practice Gratitude

Gratitude is an incredibly effective way to overcome scarcity thinking and invite abundance into your life. Each day, take a few moments to reflect on the money and financial opportunities you already have. It could be your job, your savings, the ability to pay for your essentials, or anything else you value. By focusing on what you have, rather than what you don't have, you shift your mindset from scarcity to abundance.

The practice of gratitude helps to neutralize feelings of fear, guilt, and lack, and creates a space for more abundance to flow into your life.

## Changing Unhealthy Financial Habits

In addition to money blocks, many people also struggle with unhealthy financial habits that prevent them from building wealth. These habits, if left unchecked, can sabotage your financial success and keep you stuck in a cycle of stress and frustration.

Here are some common unhealthy financial habits and how to break them:

### 1. Impulse Spending

Impulse spending is the act of buying things you don't need without thinking about the long-term consequences. It's easy to get caught up in the moment and buy things that bring temporary pleasure, but it can lead to significant financial stress over time.

To break this habit, create a **budget** and stick to it. Before making any large purchase, take a step back and ask yourself if it aligns with your long-term goals. If the purchase is unnecessary, consider waiting 24 hours before buying it, giving yourself time to reconsider.

### 2. Living Beyond Your Means

Living beyond your means is another common financial habit that can keep you trapped in debt and financial insecurity. This behavior often stems from the desire to keep up with others or to maintain a certain lifestyle, even if it's not sustainable.

To break this habit, start by tracking your expenses and finding areas where you can cut back. Eliminate any non-essential expenses and prioritize saving. Over time, you'll find that living within your means brings a sense of financial freedom and stability.

### 3. Avoiding Financial Planning

Some people avoid financial planning altogether because it feels overwhelming or they don't know where to start. However, without a financial plan, it's easy to drift aimlessly and miss out on opportunities for growth.

Start small by setting clear financial goals and creating a plan to achieve them. Whether it's paying off debt, saving for retirement, or building an emergency fund, having a plan will give you a sense of direction and help you stay focused on your financial journey.

### Conclusion

Overcoming money blocks and unhealthy financial habits is a crucial step in creating lasting financial success. By identifying and challenging your money blocks, reframing your negative thoughts, and replacing unhealthy habits with positive ones, you will unlock your true potential for wealth and abundance.

Remember, the process of transformation takes time and effort, but with consistent action and a commitment to changing your mindset and habits, you will begin to see the results in your financial life. The road to financial freedom may not always be easy, but it is worth the effort. By overcoming your money blocks and unhealthy habits, you are paving the way for a future filled with wealth, security, and peace of mind.

# Chapter 9: Building a Wealthy Mindset Through Gratitude

Gratitude is a transformative force, capable of reshaping not only how we view the world but also how we interact with it. It is often said that gratitude is the key to happiness and fulfillment, and for good reason. When practiced consciously and consistently, gratitude holds the power to shift your mindset from scarcity to abundance, from lack to wealth. In this chapter, we will explore the profound connection between gratitude and wealth-building, and how adopting daily gratitude practices can be one of the most powerful tools you use to attract financial growth.

**The Role of Gratitude in Attracting Money**

When it comes to creating wealth, the mindset you cultivate plays an immense role in determining your financial success. The way you think, feel, and act around money influences the opportunities you see, the decisions you make, and ultimately the results you get. At its core, wealth is not just about accumulating money—it is about aligning your thoughts and emotions with the energy of abundance.

Gratitude is a key player in this process. When you express gratitude, you shift your focus away from what you don't have and place your attention on what you do. This subtle shift has a profound impact on your financial life. By appreciating the money and opportunities you already have, you open yourself up to receiving more. The universe—or whatever higher power you believe in—responds to the energy you put out, and when you express gratitude, you attract more things to be grateful for.

Many successful individuals credit their wealth and success to a mindset of gratitude. They know that the more they appreciate what they already have, the more it multiplies. Gratitude is not just about being thankful for the good things in your life—it's about acknowledging that every experience, good or bad, carries a lesson that contributes to your growth. Financial abundance flows more freely when you maintain a grateful heart and a positive outlook.

The act of gratitude is a powerful magnet for wealth. This is because gratitude raises your vibration. It shifts your emotional energy from negative states, such as fear, scarcity, or resentment, to positive states, such as love, joy, and appreciation. These higher frequencies are the very same frequencies that attract wealth. Think of it as a law of attraction: the more grateful you are, the more abundance you will draw toward yourself.

Moreover, gratitude helps to rewire your subconscious mind. When you focus on being grateful for what you have, you begin to create a mental environment conducive to wealth-building. You start to notice opportunities that you might have otherwise overlooked, and you develop the confidence and optimism needed to seize them. Gratitude makes you feel abundant, even when your bank account may not yet reflect that abundance. This feeling of abundance is what ultimately leads to the manifestation of wealth.

**Daily Gratitude Practices for Financial Growth**

Gratitude is not just a concept; it's a practice. And like any practice, the more you engage in it, the more it becomes a natural part of your life. To harness the power of gratitude in attracting money and creating wealth, you must make it a daily habit. The following practices will help you integrate gratitude into your everyday life and turn it into a powerful tool for financial growth.

**1. The Gratitude Journal**

One of the most effective ways to practice gratitude is by keeping a gratitude journal. Each morning or evening, set aside a few minutes to write down at least three things you are grateful for. These can be anything from the simple joys of life, such as a delicious cup of coffee or a pleasant conversation with a friend, to more significant things, like a job opportunity or financial windfall.

The key is to focus on the positive aspects of your life, no matter how small. When you consistently record the things you are thankful for, you train your mind to focus on abundance rather than lack. Over time, you'll begin to notice more and more things to be grateful for, which in turn helps you to cultivate a mindset of abundance.

In addition to writing down what you are grateful for, consider adding specific gratitude related to your finances. For instance, you could write, "I am grateful for my steady income, which allows me to live comfortably," or "I am thankful for the opportunity to invest in my future." This reinforces the idea that your current financial situation is already a source of gratitude, and that more abundance is on its way.

**2. Gratitude Meditation**

Meditation is another powerful way to connect with the energy of gratitude. Take a few minutes each day to sit quietly, close your eyes, and focus on your breath. As you breathe, begin to visualize all the things in your life that you are grateful for. Allow the feeling of gratitude to fill your body, from your head down to your toes.

As you meditate, try to imagine the flow of money and abundance entering your life. See yourself receiving opportunities, financial gifts, and the resources you need to achieve your goals. Feel the gratitude in your heart as you embrace the idea that abundance is already on its way to you. This form of meditation helps you attune your mind to the energy of wealth and activates the law of attraction.

**3. Gratitude Affirmations**

Affirmations are positive statements that you repeat to yourself in order to reinforce a specific belief or mindset. When it comes to gratitude and wealth-building, affirmations are a powerful tool for shifting your thinking. Start each day by speaking affirmations that express gratitude for the abundance you already have and for the abundance that is on its way.

Here are some examples of gratitude affirmations related to money and financial success:

- "I am grateful for the wealth and abundance I have in my life."
- "Money flows to me easily and effortlessly, and I am thankful for it."
- "I am thankful for all the opportunities that are available to me."
- "I am grateful for the financial freedom that allows me to live life on my own terms."
- "Every day, I am attracting more and more wealth, and I am thankful for it."

As you repeat these affirmations, try to feel the emotions of gratitude and abundance. The more you feel these emotions, the more powerfully your affirmations will work. The goal is to reprogram your subconscious mind to believe that financial success and abundance are already yours.

### 4. Expressing Gratitude for Money

It might seem strange, but expressing gratitude for the money you already have, no matter how much or how little, is a powerful practice. Often, people focus on what they don't have, which perpetuates feelings of lack. Instead, make it a point to express gratitude for every dollar, rupee, or pound that enters your life.

When you receive money—whether it's from your salary, an investment, or a gift—take a moment to thank it. Say to yourself, "Thank you for this money. I appreciate you and the opportunities you bring." When you begin to view money as something to be grateful for rather than something you lack, you change your entire relationship with it. This simple practice helps you to see money as an abundant resource that flows freely into your life.

### 5. Gratitude in the Moment

Gratitude doesn't have to be reserved for your morning meditation or journaling sessions. You can practice gratitude in the moment, during your everyday activities. Whether you're paying for groceries, driving to work, or meeting with a colleague, take a few seconds to mentally acknowledge what you are grateful for in that moment.

For instance, when paying for something, think, "I'm grateful for the money that allows me to purchase this item." When driving, say to yourself, "I'm thankful for my reliable car and the ability to get where I need to go." These small moments of gratitude add up over time and help you maintain a positive mindset about money.

**Shifting Your Focus from Lack to Abundance**

The key to building wealth through gratitude lies in shifting your focus from lack to abundance. The majority of people are conditioned to focus on what they don't have—whether it's money, opportunities, or material possessions. This focus on scarcity creates feelings of fear, anxiety, and inadequacy, all of which block the flow of wealth.

By practicing gratitude consistently, you retrain your mind to focus on what you already have and what you are thankful for. When you begin to see the abundance around you, you start to realize that the universe is already providing for you. This shift in focus is incredibly powerful because it opens up space for even more abundance to flow into your life.

It's important to understand that gratitude is not about denying your desires or pretending that everything is perfect. It's about acknowledging the present moment and being thankful for what you already have while remaining open to receiving more. Gratitude shifts your focus from a mindset of "not enough" to one of "I have everything I need, and more is on its way."

**Conclusion**

Gratitude is not just a nice feeling—it is a transformative force that can change the trajectory of your financial life. By embracing daily gratitude practices and shifting your focus from lack to abundance, you create the mental and emotional conditions necessary to attract wealth and financial success.

As you integrate gratitude into your life, remember that the journey toward financial abundance is not a race, but a process. Each day, take a moment to acknowledge the blessings you have, no matter how small, and trust that more is on the way. With a grateful heart and an abundant mindset, you are well on your way to building the wealth you desire and deserve.

# Chapter 10: Creating a Vision for Your Financial Future

The journey to financial success begins with a clear and compelling vision. Without a roadmap, it's easy to get lost or distracted, but with a defined vision, you can stay focused, motivated, and on track toward achieving your financial goals. In this chapter, we will explore the importance of setting clear financial goals, how to effectively visualize your financial success, and how to map out a path to wealth and abundance.

**The Importance of Setting Clear Financial Goals**

Setting clear financial goals is the foundation of any successful financial journey. It provides you with direction, purpose, and a sense of control over your financial destiny. When you have a clear picture of where you want to go financially, you're far more likely to take the necessary steps to get there. Without this clarity, it's easy to get swept up in day-to-day concerns, distractions, and the many opportunities that present themselves—often leading to scattered efforts and a lack of progress.

Clear financial goals allow you to take deliberate action. These goals give you something to strive for, whether it's saving for a house, building a retirement fund, paying off debt, or starting a business. They help you prioritize your spending, saving, and investing, making your decisions more intentional and aligned with your long-term vision.

A well-defined goal also serves as a benchmark to measure your progress. Without clear goals, it's difficult to track how far you've come or assess whether your financial strategies are working. But when you set measurable goals, you can see your advancement and stay motivated, even when the journey seems long or difficult.

When setting financial goals, it's important to remember the SMART goal framework. SMART stands for:

- **S**pecific: The goal must be clear and detailed. Instead of saying, "I want to save money," say, "I want to save $10,000 for an emergency fund by the end of the year."
- **M**easurable: There must be a way to track your progress. In the example above, you can track the amount you've saved each month.
- **A**chievable: The goal should be realistic and attainable based on your current situation.
- **R**elevant: Your goal should align with your values and financial priorities.
- **T**ime-bound: There must be a deadline or time frame for achieving the goal.

By using the SMART framework, you create goals that are not only motivating but also actionable. Financial goals that are specific, measurable, achievable, relevant, and time-bound give you a clear path to follow and allow you to focus your efforts on the most important tasks.

**How to Visualize Your Financial Success**

Visualization is a powerful tool that can help bring your financial dreams to life. It's more than just imagining wealth—it's about creating a vivid mental picture of your financial success and feeling the emotions associated with that success. The more real and tangible your vision becomes, the more likely it is that you'll take the necessary actions to make it a reality.

Visualization works because the brain doesn't always distinguish between real and vividly imagined experiences. When you visualize success, you train your brain to believe that it is achievable, and you begin to act in ways that are consistent with that belief. When you see yourself as successful, your actions will reflect that mindset, leading you to make decisions that move you closer to your goals.

To effectively visualize your financial success, follow these steps:

1. **Find a Quiet Space:** Begin by sitting in a quiet, comfortable space where you won't be disturbed. Close your eyes and take a few deep breaths to calm your mind.

2. **Imagine Your Financial Goals:** Picture yourself living the life you want to create. What does financial success look like for you? Visualize the specific goals you want to achieve, whether it's paying off debt, buying a home, or building a thriving business. See the details—where you are, what you're doing, who's with you, and how you feel.

3. **Feel the Emotions:** As you visualize, make sure to connect with the emotions that come with achieving your financial goals. How does it feel to be debt-free, to have a secure future, or to enjoy financial freedom? The stronger the emotions, the more powerful the visualization. Feel the joy, pride, and sense of accomplishment that comes with financial success.

4. **See the Process, Not Just the End Result:** It's important to visualize not just the final outcome but the steps that will get you there. Imagine yourself taking the necessary actions: setting a budget, investing, growing your savings, or launching a business. Visualizing the process helps to solidify your commitment to the work required to achieve your goals.

5. **Practice Regularly:** Visualization is most effective when done regularly. Set aside time each day to revisit your financial vision. The more you visualize, the more it becomes ingrained in your subconscious mind. Over time, your brain will begin to look for opportunities and take actions aligned with that vision.

The key to successful visualization is consistency. Just like practicing a skill or exercising a muscle, the more you do it, the stronger your belief in your financial goals will become. Visualization reinforces the idea that your financial dreams are not only possible—they are already on their way.

### Mapping Out a Path to Wealth and Abundance

Now that you have a clear financial vision and have practiced visualization, the next step is to map out a path to get from where you are now to where you want to be. This path is your action plan—the specific steps you'll take to turn your vision into reality. Mapping out your path gives you a sense of control and direction, ensuring that you stay focused on your goals and don't get sidetracked by distractions or setbacks.

To map out your path to wealth and abundance, consider the following steps:

**1. Break Down Your Goals into Actionable Steps**

Once you've set clear financial goals, break them down into smaller, actionable steps. For example, if your goal is to save $10,000 in a year, divide it into monthly savings targets. If your goal is to invest in real estate, research potential properties, evaluate financing options, and create a plan for property acquisition. Breaking down your larger goal into smaller tasks makes it more manageable and ensures that you're consistently working toward your desired outcome.

**2. Create a Budget and Stick to It**

One of the most effective ways to stay on track with your financial goals is to create a budget. A budget helps you allocate your income to specific expenses, savings, and investments, ensuring that your money is working for you. By setting aside money for your goals each month, you make steady progress toward achieving them. Track your expenses, adjust as necessary, and stay disciplined in your spending.

**3. Invest in Your Financial Education**

To build wealth, it's essential to continuously invest in your financial knowledge. The more you learn about money management, investing, and wealth-building strategies, the better equipped you'll be to make informed decisions. Read books, take courses, and surround yourself with people who have the financial knowledge and mindset you want to adopt. The more you know, the better your decisions will be, and the faster you will progress toward your financial goals.

**4. Monitor Your Progress**

Regularly track your progress to ensure that you are on the right path. This could be monthly, quarterly, or yearly check-ins, depending on your goals. Are you meeting your savings targets? Are you sticking to your budget? Are your investments growing? If you're not on track, it's time to adjust your strategy. Financial success is not a linear path—it's an ongoing process of learning, adapting, and improving.

**5. Stay Flexible and Resilient**

Building wealth takes time, and the path to financial abundance is rarely a straight line. Unexpected expenses, changes in income, and setbacks can happen. The key is to stay flexible and resilient. If things don't go as planned, assess the situation, make adjustments, and keep moving forward. Your financial journey is unique, and resilience will help you overcome obstacles and stay focused on your ultimate goal.

**Conclusion**

Creating a vision for your financial future is not just about dreaming big—it's about setting clear goals, visualizing success, and mapping out a practical path to wealth and abundance. By following these steps and taking consistent action, you can turn your financial dreams into reality. Remember, your financial future is in your hands. With a clear vision, determination, and a commitment to growth, you have everything you need to build a prosperous and abundant life. The journey may not always be easy, but with persistence and a well-defined roadmap, you will reach your destination.

# Chapter 11: The Role of Discipline in Achieving Financial Goals

Financial success is not merely about having big dreams or setting lofty goals; it's about being disciplined enough to stay committed to those goals over the long haul. Discipline is the bridge between ambition and accomplishment. It's what turns good intentions into consistent actions and ensures that your financial vision becomes a reality. In this chapter, we will explore the role of discipline in achieving financial goals, how to cultivate financial discipline, and how to stay focused on long-term success while managing short-term desires.

**Developing Financial Discipline**

At its core, financial discipline is about self-control. It's the ability to resist temptations that might divert you from your financial goals, such as overspending, indulging in unnecessary luxuries, or falling into the trap of instant gratification. Financial discipline requires you to make conscious decisions that align with your long-term vision, rather than yielding to fleeting impulses.

To develop financial discipline, you need to first understand the difference between wants and needs. Wants are desires that may not have immediate or essential value, such as the latest smartphone, a designer handbag, or a weekend getaway. Needs, on the other hand, are essentials—things that are necessary for your survival or overall well-being, such as food, housing, and healthcare. Financial discipline involves prioritizing your needs over your wants and being mindful of where and how you allocate your resources.

One effective strategy for developing financial discipline is to create a clear, actionable budget. A budget forces you to categorize your expenses and track where your money is going. With a detailed budget, you can see whether your spending habits align with your financial goals or if you're inadvertently spending on things that don't contribute to your long-term success.

Another powerful tool for building financial discipline is setting up automatic savings or investment plans. When you automate your savings, you remove the temptation to skip a month or spend the money elsewhere. By treating savings as a non-negotiable expense, you ensure that you're consistently putting money toward your future, even when your discipline might be tested.

**How to Stay Committed to Your Financial Vision**

Staying committed to your financial vision requires more than just discipline—it also involves having a strong sense of purpose. When you know why you're pursuing a specific financial goal, whether it's building wealth for your family, achieving financial independence, or securing a comfortable retirement, it becomes easier to stay committed through the challenges.

One effective way to stay committed is to continually remind yourself of the "why" behind your goals. This can be done through visualization, affirmations, or even writing down your reasons for wanting financial success. By reconnecting with your deeper motivations, you reinforce the importance of your financial goals and maintain your drive, even when faced with distractions.

Setting smaller milestones and celebrating your progress along the way is another great strategy to stay committed. Long-term goals can feel overwhelming, but breaking them down into achievable steps makes them feel more attainable. Each time you hit a milestone, celebrate it in a way that reinforces your commitment to the larger goal. This could be as simple as acknowledging your success, treating yourself to a small reward, or reflecting on the progress you've made.

# MONEY MINDSET MASTERY

By celebrating the small wins, you build momentum and keep your motivation high.

Accountability is also key to staying committed. Find a financial accountability partner or join a community of like-minded individuals who share your goals. Having someone to share your progress with, ask for support when needed, or provide encouragement during difficult times can help you stay focused and motivated.

Lastly, stay adaptable. Life is unpredictable, and unexpected challenges can arise, forcing you to adjust your plans. Being flexible and willing to reassess your approach is a key part of maintaining commitment to your financial goals. It's important to recognize that setbacks don't mean failure—they are simply opportunities to reassess and adapt your strategies as needed. This mindset helps you stay committed even when the road to success is not as smooth as you'd like.

**Managing Short-Term Desires for Long-Term Gains**

One of the greatest tests of financial discipline is the ability to manage short-term desires in favor of long-term gains. Instant gratification is a natural human tendency, especially when it comes to spending money. The desire to splurge on an expensive meal, a new gadget, or a weekend shopping spree can often conflict with the need to save or invest for your future. In these moments, financial discipline is crucial.

To manage short-term desires, you first need to become aware of your spending triggers. For some people, shopping is an emotional release, while for others, it's about keeping up with social trends or impressing others. Identifying your personal triggers allows you to create a strategy for managing them. This might include setting limits on discretionary spending, delaying purchases to give yourself time to reconsider, or using the "24-hour rule," where you commit to waiting a full day before making any non-essential purchases. This simple strategy can help you avoid impulsive decisions that might derail your financial goals.

Another effective approach is to reframe your thinking about money. Instead of seeing savings and investments as sacrifices, view them as investments in your future freedom and peace of mind. Imagine the financial security that comes with a fully-funded emergency fund, a growing investment portfolio, or a debt-free life. By shifting your perspective, you begin to see short-term sacrifices not as deprivation, but as strategic decisions that will lead to greater rewards in the long run.

Visualizing your future success is another powerful tool in managing short-term desires. When faced with the temptation to spend, imagine how much closer you'll be to your financial goals if you resist. Visualize the satisfaction of watching your savings grow or the freedom of having enough money to cover your retirement expenses. Keeping this vision of your future self in mind makes it easier to resist the pull of short-term desires.

It's also helpful to establish a healthy balance between enjoying the present and planning for the future. Financial discipline doesn't mean depriving yourself entirely of fun or enjoyment; it's about finding a middle ground where you can live within your means while also making smart choices for your financial future. Allocate a portion of your income for enjoyment—whether it's a night out, a hobby, or a small luxury—so that you don't feel like you're constantly depriving yourself. The key is moderation and balance.

One of the most powerful ways to manage short-term desires is by developing a strong "why" for your financial goals. When you are deeply connected to the purpose behind your efforts—whether it's the desire for financial freedom, the ability to give generously, or the ability to live a comfortable life—you are far less likely to be swayed by the temporary pleasures that can derail your progress.

**Developing Good Financial Habits**

Building discipline also means developing good financial habits that become automatic and ingrained in your daily life. These habits help to eliminate the need for constant decision-making and reduce the temptation to spend impulsively. Here are some habits that will help you develop stronger financial discipline:

- **Track your spending:** Regularly monitor where your money is going. This can help you identify areas where you can cut back or make more intentional choices about how you allocate your resources.
- **Automate savings and investments:** Set up automatic transfers to your savings and investment accounts so that you prioritize these contributions before anything else.
- **Create and stick to a budget:** A detailed budget allows you to allocate money for your needs, wants, and financial goals, making it easier to stick to your financial plan.
- **Avoid high-interest debt:** Be mindful of taking on high-interest debt that can eat into your financial future. Pay off existing debt as quickly as possible, starting with high-interest balances.
- **Reinvest earnings:** As you begin to generate wealth, reinvest your earnings to compound your returns and accelerate your financial growth.

**Conclusion**

Financial discipline is the cornerstone of wealth-building. It's the difference between dreaming about financial freedom and actually achieving it. By developing financial discipline, staying committed to your financial vision, and learning how to manage short-term desires, you can transform your financial future. It's not about being perfect or making no mistakes—it's about making consistent, intentional decisions that align with your long-term goals. Discipline is not a restriction; it's the key to unlocking the abundant future you deserve. By practicing these principles and making them a part of your daily life, you'll find that financial success is not just a distant dream, but an achievable reality.

# Chapter 12: Investing in Yourself: The Best Path to Wealth

When most people think about building wealth, they envision stocks, real estate, or business ventures. But there's one investment that is often overlooked—yet it holds the greatest potential for long-term success: **investing in yourself.** Self-investment isn't just about spending money on courses or reading books; it's a mindset, a commitment to growth, and a powerful driver of wealth creation. In this chapter, we will explore why investing in yourself is the best path to wealth, how you can develop the skills and knowledge needed for financial growth, and how leveraging education and personal development can set you on the path to success.

### The Importance of Self-Investment

The idea of investing in yourself is simple: the more you grow as an individual, the more capable you become of generating wealth, seizing opportunities, and creating lasting value. Whether it's gaining new skills, expanding your knowledge, or building your emotional intelligence, every form of personal development increases your value in the world. When you improve your ability to contribute, to solve problems, and to think strategically, you inevitably increase your potential to create wealth, achieve financial independence, and lead a successful life.

Investing in yourself is not just about the tangible skills you gain; it's also about cultivating the right mindset. A mindset that sees learning as a lifelong pursuit, that welcomes challenges as opportunities for growth, and that values the journey of self-improvement. This mindset will serve as the foundation for all your future endeavors, both personally and financially.

Self-investment is unique because it delivers returns that no external investment can match. When you invest in your personal growth, you build a more resilient, adaptable, and innovative version of yourself. Whether you're acquiring new skills, improving your mental and emotional health, or broadening your perspective on the world, the dividends of self-investment are profound. They not only benefit your career and financial success but also lead to a richer, more fulfilling life overall.

### How to Develop Skills and Knowledge for Financial Growth

Building wealth isn't just about making money; it's about **becoming the kind of person who can create, manage, and grow wealth**. The foundation of this transformation is the acquisition of valuable skills and knowledge that allow you to operate at a higher level and unlock greater opportunities. But how do you develop these skills and knowledge?

**1. Invest in Education: Formal and Informal Learning**

Education is a powerful tool for increasing your earning potential and enhancing your financial growth. You don't necessarily need to have a formal degree to achieve wealth, but learning how to acquire knowledge effectively can give you the tools to succeed. Education can take many forms, and it's up to you to choose which path suits your goals.

- **Formal Education:** For some, going back to school or pursuing a degree is the right step. A college education or a specialized certification can open doors to lucrative careers, whether in business, finance, technology, or healthcare. Education provides not only knowledge but also valuable networking opportunities and credibility.

- **Self-Education:** The beauty of the digital age is that education is more accessible than ever. From online courses, podcasts, and YouTube videos to books, webinars, and masterclasses, the opportunities for self-education are vast. Investing in a course on finance, marketing, or entrepreneurship could be a game-changer for your financial future. But it's not just about quantity; it's about quality. Choose resources that provide you with practical, actionable knowledge that you can immediately apply to your financial life.

**2. Master a High-Income Skill**

One of the most effective ways to invest in yourself is by mastering a high-income skill. A high-income skill is any skill that allows you to generate significant income, often because there is demand for it in the marketplace. Some high-income skills are technical, like coding, data analysis, and digital marketing. Others are creative, like writing, graphic design, and video production. Still, others are more relational, like sales and negotiation.

The key to developing a high-income skill is consistency and practice. You need to dedicate time every day to learning, practicing, and improving. Whether it's coding, copywriting, or becoming a financial analyst, mastery comes with time and effort. As you grow more proficient, your ability to command higher pay and more opportunities will naturally follow.

**3. Learn Financial Literacy**

No matter how successful you become in your career, if you don't understand how money works, your wealth-building efforts will be limited. Financial literacy is the cornerstone of financial success. It's the ability to manage, grow, and multiply your money through sound decision-making. Learning how to budget, save, invest, and plan for taxes is crucial to your financial health.

Investing in financial education can be as simple as reading books on money management, listening to podcasts, or attending seminars on investing. The more you understand about the financial world—stocks, bonds, real estate, cryptocurrency, and other wealth-building vehicles—the better prepared you'll be to grow your wealth. Financial literacy empowers you to make smarter decisions with your money and to seize opportunities that others may overlook.

### 4. Develop Emotional Intelligence (EQ)

Emotional intelligence (EQ) is the ability to understand and manage your emotions and the emotions of others. It's a critical skill in both personal and professional life, especially when it comes to building wealth. People with high EQ are better at networking, negotiating, and leading teams, all of which can contribute to financial success.

Investing in your emotional intelligence involves learning how to regulate your emotions, practice empathy, communicate effectively, and resolve conflicts. As your EQ improves, so does your ability to navigate complex social and professional situations, leading to more success in business and finance.

### 5. Cultivate Entrepreneurial Thinking

Even if you don't own a business, thinking like an entrepreneur can significantly enhance your wealth-building journey. Entrepreneurs see opportunities where others see obstacles. They are comfortable taking calculated risks, they innovate, and they constantly seek ways to create value. Cultivating an entrepreneurial mindset involves thinking outside the box, being resourceful, and developing a problem-solving attitude.

You don't have to start a business right away, but practicing entrepreneurial thinking in your career, investments, and daily life can open doors to wealth. By being proactive, taking initiative, and identifying opportunities for improvement, you can create additional income streams, develop new skills, and stay ahead of the curve in an ever-changing world.

### Leveraging Education and Personal Development for Success

Education and personal development are two sides of the same coin. While education equips you with the technical skills and knowledge to succeed, personal development ensures you have the mindset, emotional resilience, and character to handle challenges and seize opportunities.

To leverage education for success, you must first create a plan. Identify the skills and knowledge you need to achieve your financial goals and seek out the resources that will help you acquire them. Whether it's taking a course on investing, reading books on entrepreneurship, or attending workshops on leadership, make self-education a priority.

But education alone isn't enough. Personal development is equally important. It's about building the habits, mindset, and behaviors that support your growth. This includes developing discipline, cultivating a positive attitude, managing stress, and staying focused on your goals. Personal development is the foundation upon which your education will thrive.

**The Compounding Effect of Self-Investment**

The beauty of investing in yourself is that the returns are compounded over time. Just as you can earn compound interest on your investments, you can experience compounded growth as you continue to invest in your skills, knowledge, and personal development. Each new skill, piece of knowledge, or mindset shift adds value to your life and sets you up for greater success in the future.

Over time, the effects of self-investment compound, making you a more capable, valuable, and successful person. Your earning potential increases, your career opportunities multiply, and your ability to navigate life's challenges becomes stronger. The more you invest in yourself, the greater the returns—and the sooner you'll realize the wealth you've been building, not just financially, but in every area of your life.

**Conclusion**

Investing in yourself is the best path to wealth because it's an investment that pays unlimited dividends. By acquiring new skills, expanding your knowledge, and cultivating a strong mindset, you position yourself to seize opportunities, overcome obstacles, and create lasting success. Whether you're learning how to invest, developing a high-income skill, or improving your emotional intelligence, every step you take toward personal growth is a step toward financial abundance. The more you invest in yourself, the more you increase your ability to create wealth, not just for today, but for the future as well. Your most valuable asset is you—so invest wisely, and watch your wealth and success grow.

# Chapter 13: Creating Multiple Streams of Income

In today's volatile economy, relying on a single source of income has become increasingly risky. Job security is a concept that has all but disappeared for many people, and even those with steady careers are discovering that having only one stream of income is no longer sufficient for financial security. The key to building lasting wealth is to create multiple streams of income—each one contributing to your financial freedom and stability. This chapter will delve into why relying on one income source is risky, how to create passive income streams, and share real-world examples of successful entrepreneurs who have mastered the art of generating multiple income streams.

**Why Relying on One Source of Income Is Risky**

For many years, the traditional model of working for a single employer and relying on a paycheck was considered the securest path to financial stability. However, this is no longer the case. The rise of automation, the gig economy, and economic uncertainty has made the concept of a "single job for life" obsolete. Here are a few reasons why relying on one source of income is risky in today's world:

**1. Job Insecurity**

Job security is becoming increasingly rare. Companies are restructuring, downsizing, or outsourcing jobs to reduce costs. Even long-term employees with decades of experience are finding themselves laid off due to unforeseen circumstances, such as economic recessions or technological advancements. In an unpredictable job market, losing your job without any alternative income streams can lead to financial instability and stress.

**2. Income Stagnation**

If your only income comes from your job or business, your financial growth will often be limited by factors like salary caps, inflation, or business cycles. Even if you receive annual raises, they may not keep up with the rising cost of living. Without other sources of income, you may find it difficult to increase your wealth or achieve your financial goals at the pace you desire.

**3. Limited Wealth-Building Opportunities**

Having a single income stream often leaves you in a position where you're living paycheck to paycheck. Without extra income, it becomes nearly impossible to build wealth through investments, save for future goals, or take calculated risks with your finances. Multiple income streams not only provide you with more financial resources but also allow you to diversify your wealth-building efforts, which ultimately leads to faster wealth accumulation.

**4. Unforeseen Life Events**

Life is unpredictable. An illness, accident, or family emergency could require you to take time off work or force you to stop working altogether. In such cases, depending solely on a single income source could leave you financially vulnerable. Having multiple streams of income provides a safety net in the event that something unforeseen occurs and one of your income sources is interrupted.

**5. Lack of Control**

When you rely on one source of income—whether from an employer or a single business—you are dependent on the decisions and circumstances beyond your control. An employer can decide to lay you off at any time. Similarly, if your business depends on a few clients or customers, a loss of those clients could be catastrophic. Multiple streams of income offer you more control over your financial future and allow you to adapt to changes in the marketplace.

# MONEY MINDSET MASTERY

## How to Create Passive Income Streams

While actively working for money is a necessity for many people, building **passive income** is the key to achieving financial freedom. Passive income refers to money earned with minimal active involvement, often after an initial effort or investment. Here are several ways you can create passive income streams that will work for you over time.

### 1. Investing in Real Estate

One of the most popular and effective ways to build passive income is through real estate investment. By purchasing rental properties, you can earn regular income through rent payments. Over time, these properties may also appreciate in value, providing long-term capital gains when sold.

However, real estate investment does require upfront capital and knowledge of the market. You'll need to research potential properties, secure financing, and manage tenants or hire property management. But once the systems are in place, it can be a reliable source of passive income.

For those who don't want to manage properties directly, Real Estate Investment Trusts (REITs) allow you to invest in a portfolio of properties and receive dividends without the hands-on responsibilities.

### 2. Dividend Stocks and Bonds

Investing in dividend-paying stocks or bonds is another excellent way to create passive income. Dividend stocks are shares in companies that distribute a portion of their profits to shareholders on a regular basis. By carefully selecting high-quality dividend stocks, you can generate a steady stream of income, which can grow as the company increases its payouts.

Similarly, bonds—whether corporate or government-issued—provide regular interest payments. While bonds are generally considered less risky than stocks, they typically offer lower returns. Combining dividend stocks with bonds allows for a diversified and more secure passive income strategy.

### 3. Create and Sell Digital Products

The digital world has opened up vast opportunities for generating passive income. One of the easiest ways to create a passive income stream is by developing and selling digital products. These can include:

- **E-books:** Write an e-book on a subject you're passionate about or an area where you have expertise. Once it's written, you can sell it on platforms like Amazon Kindle, making money every time someone downloads a copy.

- **Online Courses:** If you have a specialized skill or knowledge in a specific area, consider creating an online course. Websites like Udemy and Teachable allow you to create, market, and sell courses to a global audience. Once created, the course can generate sales passively.

- **Digital Art or Photography:** For artists or photographers, selling digital versions of your work online through platforms like Etsy, Shutterstock, or Adobe Stock can generate ongoing passive income.

- **Software or Apps:** If you're technically inclined, developing software or mobile apps can provide a lucrative source of passive income. After development and launch, the product can be sold or monetized through ads or subscriptions.

### 4. Affiliate Marketing

Affiliate marketing is another powerful passive income stream. In affiliate marketing, you promote products or services offered by other companies through your website, blog, or social media. When someone purchases the product or service using your unique affiliate link, you earn a commission.

To be successful in affiliate marketing, you need to have a platform with traffic, such as a blog, YouTube channel, or Instagram account. Once you've built an audience and established trust, affiliate marketing can provide a consistent stream of passive income.

## MONEY MINDSET MASTERY

**5. Peer-to-Peer Lending and Crowdfunding**

Peer-to-peer lending platforms, like LendingClub or Prosper, allow you to lend money to individuals or small businesses in exchange for interest payments. As the lender, you can choose the loan terms and earn interest over time as the borrower repays the loan. This can be a great way to earn passive income, though it comes with risks, such as the potential for borrower defaults.

Crowdfunding platforms, like Kickstarter and Indiegogo, allow you to invest in new ideas and products, often with the opportunity to receive early access to the product or shares in the business. These investments can generate returns if the business succeeds, though they carry significant risk.

### Real-World Examples of Successful Entrepreneurs

Many successful entrepreneurs have created multiple streams of income, and their stories can serve as inspiration for those looking to build wealth. Below are a few examples of individuals who have diversified their income and built wealth through multiple sources.

**1. Robert Kiyosaki**

Robert Kiyosaki, the author of the bestselling book *Rich Dad Poor Dad*, is a perfect example of someone who understands the importance of creating multiple income streams. In addition to his writing and speaking career, Kiyosaki has built wealth through real estate investments, business ventures, and the creation of educational products. His philosophy emphasizes financial education, entrepreneurship, and the importance of building passive income sources.

**2. Grant Cardone**

Grant Cardone is a successful entrepreneur, author, and motivational speaker who has created multiple income streams through real estate, business ventures, and sales training. His investment strategy includes purchasing multifamily properties and commercial real estate, which generate cash flow and long-term wealth. Cardone's businesses, books, and online courses also provide additional streams of income. He often speaks about the importance of diversifying your income sources to avoid relying on any single stream.

### 3. Sara Blakely

Sara Blakely, the founder of Spanx, is a prime example of an entrepreneur who has created multiple streams of income through her brand. While her primary income comes from the sales of Spanx, Blakely has also invested in real estate and other businesses. She has leveraged her success to invest in various ventures, building an empire that continues to grow.

### 4. Elon Musk

Elon Musk, the founder of Tesla, SpaceX, and several other companies, is a living example of someone who has multiple income streams. Through his various companies, Musk generates significant income from product sales, government contracts, and other ventures. He also has stakes in several other companies, including SolarCity, which has helped diversify his wealth-building strategies.

### Conclusion

Creating multiple streams of income is a crucial strategy for building wealth and achieving financial security. Relying on a single income source exposes you to unnecessary risk, whereas diversifying your income can provide stability, increase wealth-building opportunities, and ensure long-term financial success. By exploring passive income opportunities such as real estate, dividend stocks, digital products, affiliate marketing, and lending, you can create multiple income streams that work for you even while you sleep. Follow the examples of successful entrepreneurs who have mastered the art of income diversification, and begin taking steps today to create your own wealth-building strategy. The future of your financial freedom lies in your ability to build multiple streams of income—and the sooner you start, the sooner you'll reap the rewards.

# Chapter 14: Money Management: Practical Strategies for Wealth Building

Money management is often the make-or-break factor in your journey to financial success. Many people accumulate money without ever learning how to manage it effectively, which leads to financial instability and missed opportunities. Managing your money wisely is not just about saving—it's about making informed decisions that help you grow your wealth, achieve your goals, and secure your financial future. In this chapter, we will explore practical strategies for money management, the 50/30/20 rule and other financial strategies, and how to prioritize savings and investments.

### The Importance of Money Management

Money management is the foundation upon which financial success is built. The decisions you make regarding how you spend, save, and invest your money directly influence the outcome of your financial future. Good money management allows you to maintain a healthy financial lifestyle, make progress toward your financial goals, and avoid the pitfalls that can lead to debt or financial ruin.

Without proper management, even high incomes can be squandered, leading to stress, instability, and missed opportunities for wealth building. Conversely, those who master money management often find themselves ahead of the curve, with increasing wealth and financial security.

Effective money management requires discipline, self-awareness, and a structured approach. Here are the foundational principles that will guide you on your journey:

**1. Track Your Income and Expenses**

The first step in managing your money wisely is understanding where it is coming from and where it is going. You cannot begin to build wealth if you do not have a clear picture of your finances. Tracking your income and expenses gives you visibility into your financial situation and helps you identify areas where you can cut back or allocate more toward savings or investments.

Start by keeping a detailed record of all sources of income, including your salary, freelance work, and any passive income streams. Then, track your expenses. This includes everything from rent or mortgage payments, utilities, food, transportation, insurance, entertainment, and discretionary spending. Use a budgeting app or spreadsheet to categorize your expenses so you can see where your money is going.

Once you have a clear understanding of your income and spending habits, you will be in a better position to make changes and allocate your resources more efficiently.

**2. Create a Budget**

The next step in money management is to create a budget. A budget is essentially a plan for how you will allocate your income to cover your expenses, savings, and investments. Having a budget ensures that you are living within your means, preventing overspending, and helping you make consistent progress toward your financial goals.

There are many ways to approach budgeting, but one of the most popular and effective methods is the **50/30/20 rule**. This simple rule divides your income into three categories:

- **50% for Needs:** This includes essential expenses such as rent or mortgage, utilities, food, healthcare, and transportation. These are the non-negotiable costs you need to live and work.
- **30% for Wants:** These are discretionary expenses like entertainment, dining out, shopping, and vacations. While not essential, these expenses enhance your quality of life.

- **20% for Savings and Investments:** This portion of your income should be set aside for building wealth. Ideally, 20% of your income should go toward building an emergency fund, saving for retirement, and investing in assets that will generate future income.

By following the 50/30/20 rule, you can ensure that you are not only covering your basic needs and wants but also prioritizing wealth building and financial security.

While the 50/30/20 rule is a great starting point, it can be adjusted to better fit your personal financial situation. For example, if you have significant debt, you may want to allocate a higher percentage of your income toward paying it off. Or, if you're aggressively saving for a goal, you might want to reduce your discretionary spending.

### 3. Implement the Zero-Based Budgeting Method

Another effective strategy for money management is **zero-based budgeting**, which involves allocating every dollar of your income to a specific expense or savings goal, leaving you with a "zero balance" at the end of the month. This method forces you to be intentional with every dollar, ensuring that your money is working toward your financial objectives.

With zero-based budgeting, you start by calculating your total income for the month. Then, allocate that income to every expense, including savings and investments, until the entire amount is accounted for. This method helps eliminate wasteful spending and ensures that you're fully utilizing your resources to achieve your goals.

### 4. Prioritize Savings and Investments

One of the most crucial aspects of money management is making savings and investments a priority. Building wealth isn't just about earning more money—it's about keeping a portion of that money and putting it to work for you.

Start by building an emergency fund. An emergency fund is money set aside for unexpected expenses, such as medical bills, car repairs, or job loss. Aim to save three to six months' worth of living expenses in a liquid, easily accessible account, such as a savings account. Having an emergency fund gives you peace of mind and ensures that you won't be forced into debt when life throws you a curveball.

Once your emergency fund is in place, it's time to focus on building wealth through investments. The earlier you start investing, the more time your money has to grow. Begin by contributing to retirement accounts, such as a 401(k) or an IRA, which offer tax advantages. As you become more comfortable with investing, consider diversifying into stocks, bonds, mutual funds, real estate, and other wealth-building vehicles.

### Effective Strategies for Managing Money

Now that we've covered the foundational aspects of money management, let's explore some additional practical strategies that can help you optimize your financial health and accelerate your wealth-building journey.

### 1. Avoid Lifestyle Inflation

As your income increases, it's tempting to increase your spending as well. This is called **lifestyle inflation**, and it's one of the most common reasons people fail to build wealth. Just because you get a raise or start earning more money doesn't mean you should immediately upgrade your lifestyle.

Instead, focus on keeping your living expenses relatively stable as your income grows. Use the additional income to increase your savings rate, pay off debt, or invest in assets. By avoiding lifestyle inflation, you can build wealth much faster and achieve financial independence sooner.

### 2. Pay Yourself First

One of the most effective strategies for building wealth is the concept of **paying yourself first**. This means that as soon as you receive your income, you set aside money for savings and investments before spending anything on bills or discretionary expenses.

By paying yourself first, you ensure that saving and investing become non-negotiable priorities in your budget. This strategy can be especially effective if you automate your savings by setting up automatic transfers to your savings or investment accounts. Once the money is out of your checking account and into your savings or investments, you won't be tempted to spend it on non-essential items.

**3. Track Your Progress**

It's important to track your financial progress regularly to ensure that you're staying on track toward your goals. This involves reviewing your budget, savings, investments, and net worth on a monthly or quarterly basis. By monitoring your progress, you can identify any areas where you may need to adjust your spending or increase your savings rate.

Regular tracking helps you stay accountable and focused on your financial goals. If you find that you're falling behind, use the data to make informed decisions about where to cut back or allocate more resources to catch up.

**4. Eliminate Debt**

Debt is one of the biggest obstacles to wealth building, and it's essential to tackle it head-on. Begin by identifying your high-interest debts, such as credit card debt, and focus on paying them off as quickly as possible. High-interest debt can eat away at your wealth-building efforts, so getting rid of it should be a top priority.

Once your high-interest debt is cleared, focus on paying off other debts, such as student loans or mortgages. The sooner you eliminate debt, the more resources you'll have available to invest and grow your wealth.

**5. Make Smart Tax Decisions**

Tax planning is a key aspect of effective money management. The more you understand how taxes work, the better you can structure your finances to minimize your tax liability and keep more of your hard-earned money.

Take advantage of tax-advantaged accounts like retirement plans, health savings accounts (HSAs), and flexible spending accounts (FSAs). These accounts allow you to defer taxes or even avoid them altogether, which helps maximize your savings and investment returns.

Additionally, consider working with a tax professional to ensure that you're making the most tax-efficient decisions regarding your income, deductions, and investments.

**Conclusion**

Effective money management is the cornerstone of wealth building. It requires discipline, strategic planning, and a long-term mindset. By tracking your income and expenses, creating a budget, prioritizing savings and investments, and implementing effective financial strategies, you can take control of your financial future and start building lasting wealth.

The 50/30/20 rule is a great starting point for managing your money wisely, but don't be afraid to adjust it to fit your unique financial situation. Whether you're paying off debt, saving for retirement, or investing in assets, the key is to be intentional with your money and make decisions that align with your long-term goals.

Remember, building wealth doesn't happen overnight. It requires patience, persistence, and a commitment to your financial future. By adopting smart money management strategies, you'll put yourself in the best position to achieve financial freedom and live the life you've always dreamed of.

# Chapter 15: Overcoming Debt and Building Credit

Debt is a financial burden that can hold people back from achieving their full potential. It can be a significant source of stress, affecting everything from personal relationships to overall happiness. But while debt may feel like an insurmountable obstacle, with the right approach and mindset, it can be overcome. Understanding the difference between good and bad debt, employing practical strategies to get out of debt, and building a strong credit score are essential steps in gaining financial freedom and building a solid foundation for long-term wealth.

**Understanding Good vs. Bad Debt**

Not all debt is created equal. The distinction between good and bad debt is critical in shaping your financial future. It's essential to understand how different types of debt impact your finances so that you can make informed decisions and avoid falling into financial traps.

**Good Debt**

Good debt is typically associated with investments that will increase in value over time or provide long-term benefits. It can help you build wealth and improve your financial standing. Common examples of good debt include:

1. **Student Loans**: While taking on student loans can feel daunting, education is an investment in your future. A college degree or specialized training can lead to higher-paying job opportunities and career advancement, making the debt worth taking on. However, it's

crucial to borrow wisely and ensure that the degree or program you pursue aligns with a stable and lucrative career.

2. **Mortgage Debt**: Purchasing a home can be one of the most significant financial decisions you'll make. A mortgage is considered good debt if it allows you to build equity in a property that is likely to appreciate over time. Owning a home can provide long-term financial stability and create wealth, especially when property values rise. However, it's essential to make sure the mortgage payment fits within your budget and that you aren't taking on more than you can afford.

3. **Business Loans**: Taking on debt to invest in a business can be a form of good debt, especially if the loan allows you to generate revenue and expand your business. Business loans help entrepreneurs grow and scale their ventures, potentially leading to greater wealth creation. However, just as with any investment, success depends on careful planning, market research, and financial management.

4. **Investment Loans**: Some people take out loans to invest in assets that generate passive income, such as real estate properties or stocks. When used wisely, investment loans can leverage your capital and accelerate wealth-building. For example, if you purchase rental property and generate consistent rental income, the return on investment can exceed the cost of the loan, making it a smart financial move.

**Bad Debt**

Bad debt, on the other hand, refers to debt that doesn't offer long-term benefits and is usually associated with depreciating assets or unnecessary purchases. It can drain your finances and prevent you from building wealth. Common examples of bad debt include:

1. **Credit Card Debt**: High-interest credit card debt is one of the most dangerous forms of bad debt. Many people accumulate credit card debt by financing purchases they cannot afford. Credit card interest rates can be sky-high, making it difficult to pay off balances,

especially if you're only making the minimum payments. Over time, this can snowball into a massive amount of debt that seems impossible to pay off.

2. **Personal Loans for Non-Essential Purchases**: Taking out loans for vacations, luxury items, or other non-essential expenses can create financial strain without providing lasting value. While personal loans may seem like an easy way to fund indulgent purchases, they can quickly lead to financial problems when you cannot afford the repayments.

3. **Car Loans**: While buying a car may seem like a necessary expense, auto loans are typically considered bad debt because cars depreciate quickly. Unlike real estate, a car doesn't appreciate in value over time, and taking on an auto loan for a vehicle that you cannot afford can put you in financial jeopardy.

4. **Payday Loans**: Payday loans are short-term loans that come with extremely high-interest rates, often leading to a cycle of debt. These loans are designed to be repaid quickly but can trap borrowers in debt if they cannot repay on time. Payday loans should be avoided whenever possible.

While some types of debt are necessary and can be used strategically to improve your financial position, bad debt can hinder your ability to build wealth and achieve financial freedom. Identifying bad debt and eliminating it should be a primary goal on your journey to financial stability.

### Practical Strategies for Getting Out of Debt

Now that we've identified good and bad debt, let's look at practical strategies to help you get out of debt and regain control of your finances. Overcoming debt is not an overnight process, but with consistent effort and the right mindset, you can work your way out of financial obligations and into a position where you can save, invest, and build wealth.

## 1. Create a Debt Repayment Plan

One of the first steps in eliminating debt is to create a debt repayment plan. This plan should outline your current debts, the interest rates, minimum payments, and any other relevant information. Knowing the full extent of your debt will give you a clear picture of where you stand financially and allow you to make strategic decisions about how to pay it off.

There are two common methods for paying down debt:

- **Debt Snowball Method**: With the debt snowball method, you focus on paying off the smallest debt first, regardless of the interest rate. Once the smallest debt is paid off, you move to the next smallest, and so on. This method provides a psychological boost as you see debts disappearing, motivating you to keep going.
- **Debt Avalanche Method**: In the debt avalanche method, you focus on paying off the debt with the highest interest rate first. Once the high-interest debt is paid off, you move on to the next highest interest rate. This method saves you more money in interest payments over time but can be slower at first.

Choose the method that works best for you based on your personality and financial situation. Some people find the snowball method more motivating, while others prefer the avalanche method for its financial efficiency.

## 2. Cut Back on Expenses

One of the most effective ways to pay off debt is to free up extra cash by cutting back on unnecessary expenses. Look at your budget and identify areas where you can reduce spending, such as eating out, entertainment, or subscription services. Redirect the money saved into paying off your debt faster.

This might require making temporary sacrifices, but the long-term benefits will outweigh the short-term discomfort. Focus on needs rather than wants, and prioritize paying off debt over lifestyle upgrades.

### 3. Increase Your Income

In addition to cutting back on expenses, increasing your income can help you pay off debt more quickly. Look for opportunities to earn extra money, such as:
- Taking on a part-time job or side hustle
- Freelancing in your area of expertise
- Selling unused items around your home
- Monetizing a skill, such as tutoring or consulting

The extra income can be used exclusively to pay down debt, helping you become debt-free faster and with less financial stress.

### 4. Consolidate or Refinance Your Debt

If you have multiple high-interest debts, consider consolidating them into a single loan with a lower interest rate. Debt consolidation allows you to simplify your payments by combining several debts into one monthly payment, often with a lower interest rate. This can make your debt more manageable and reduce the total interest you pay over time.

If consolidation isn't an option, refinancing your debt—especially credit card debt or loans—can also help reduce your interest rates and lower your monthly payments.

### 5. Negotiate with Creditors

In some cases, negotiating with creditors can result in reduced payments or even a partial reduction of the total amount owed. Creditors may be willing to work with you if you explain your financial situation and show a commitment to repaying the debt.

If you have several months of missed payments or high-interest rates, reaching out to creditors to negotiate lower interest rates or settlements can help you get back on track.

### Building and Maintaining a Strong Credit Score

Your credit score is a reflection of your financial behavior, and it plays a significant role in your ability to borrow money, secure loans, and even rent an apartment. A strong credit score opens doors to favorable loan terms, lower interest rates, and better financial opportunities. On the other hand, a poor credit score can make it difficult to get approved for loans or credit, and when you are approved, it will likely come with higher interest rates.

**1. Understand How Credit Scores Work**

Credit scores range from 300 to 850, with higher scores indicating better creditworthiness. Your score is determined by several factors, including:

- **Payment History (35%)**: On-time payments are the most significant factor in determining your credit score. Late or missed payments can negatively impact your score, while timely payments help improve it.
- **Credit Utilization (30%)**: This refers to the ratio of your credit card balances to your credit limits. Keeping your credit utilization below 30% is ideal for maintaining a healthy credit score.
- **Length of Credit History (15%)**: The longer you have a credit history, the better your score will be. This is why it's important to keep old accounts open, even if you don't use them frequently.
- **Types of Credit Used (10%)**: Having a mix of credit accounts—credit cards, loans, mortgages—can benefit your credit score, as long as you manage them responsibly.
- **New Credit (10%)**: Opening multiple new credit accounts in a short period can lower your score, as it may suggest that you are taking on too much debt.

**2. Improve Your Credit Score**

If your credit score needs improvement, take proactive steps to raise it:

- **Pay bills on time**: Consistently paying your bills on time is the most important factor in maintaining a good credit score. Set reminders or automate payments to ensure you never miss a due date.

- **Reduce credit card debt**: Pay down credit card balances to keep your credit utilization ratio low. The lower your balances relative to your limits, the better your score will be.
- **Don't apply for too much new credit**: Opening multiple credit accounts in a short period can hurt your score. Only apply for new credit when absolutely necessary.
- **Check your credit report for errors**: Review your credit report regularly to ensure there are no errors or fraudulent activities. Dispute any inaccuracies to keep your score intact.

### 3. Maintain a Strong Credit Score

Once you've built a strong credit score, it's important to maintain it. Continue making timely payments, keep credit utilization low, and avoid unnecessary credit inquiries. Maintaining good credit will open doors to better financing options and help you achieve your financial goals.

**Conclusion**

Overcoming debt and building a strong credit score is a vital component of financial success. By understanding the difference between good and bad debt, creating a solid debt repayment plan, and employing effective strategies to get out of debt, you can regain control of your finances. Additionally, building and maintaining a good credit score will provide you with greater financial opportunities and a strong foundation for wealth building.

Remember, overcoming debt is not an overnight process—it takes time, discipline, and persistence. But with a well-executed plan, you can break free from the weight of debt and build a brighter, more secure financial future.

# Chapter 16: Wealth Building through Smart Investing

Investing is one of the most powerful tools for building long-term wealth. While saving money is important, it is through investing that you can create significant financial growth. However, investing is often misunderstood, and many people shy away from it due to fear or lack of knowledge. Understanding the basics of investing, the power of compounding interest, and how to start investing with small amounts of money are essential steps to building wealth through smart investing.

**Understanding the Basics of Investing**

Investing is the act of allocating money or resources into something that will yield a return over time. The goal of investing is to generate income or profit through capital appreciation, dividends, or interest. Whether you're investing in stocks, bonds, real estate, or other assets, the fundamental principle remains the same: invest with the expectation of a financial return.

**Types of Investments**

Before you can start investing, it's important to understand the different types of investments available. Here are some of the most common investment options:

1. **Stocks**: When you invest in stocks, you're buying ownership in a company. Stockholders are entitled to a portion of the company's profits, often in the form of dividends, and may benefit from price appreciation as the company grows and becomes more profitable. Stocks are typically more volatile than other investments, meaning their value can fluctuate dramatically in the short term. However, over

the long term, stocks have historically provided higher returns than most other asset classes.

2. **Bonds**: Bonds are essentially loans that you make to companies or governments in exchange for periodic interest payments. When you buy a bond, you are lending money to the issuer for a set period, after which the principal is returned. Bonds are generally considered safer investments than stocks, but they offer lower returns. They can be an excellent option for those seeking stability and regular income.

3. **Real Estate**: Real estate investing involves purchasing property, such as residential or commercial real estate, with the goal of generating income through rent or capital appreciation. Real estate can be an excellent way to diversify your investment portfolio, as property values tend to increase over time. Additionally, rental properties provide a steady income stream. However, real estate investing requires more initial capital and can involve significant maintenance and management costs.

4. **Mutual Funds and ETFs**: Mutual funds and exchange-traded funds (ETFs) pool money from multiple investors to invest in a diversified portfolio of stocks, bonds, or other assets. Mutual funds are actively managed by a fund manager, while ETFs are typically passively managed and track a specific index, like the S&P 500. Both types of funds provide investors with diversification and lower risk compared to individual stocks, making them an excellent choice for beginners.

5. **Cryptocurrency**: Cryptocurrency is a relatively new form of investment that involves digital currencies such as Bitcoin, Ethereum, and others. Cryptocurrencies can be highly volatile, making them risky but potentially very profitable. Some investors view cryptocurrency as a hedge against inflation or as an alternative asset class, while others are cautious due to its speculative nature.

6. **Precious Metals**: Investing in precious metals like gold, silver, and platinum is another way to diversify your investment portfolio. Precious metals tend to retain their value during times of economic

uncertainty, and they can act as a hedge against inflation. While they may not offer the same growth potential as stocks or real estate, they can be a stable part of a well-rounded investment strategy.

### Risk and Reward

All investments come with a certain level of risk, and the level of risk you are willing to take on will determine the types of investments you make. In general, higher-risk investments offer the potential for higher returns, but they also come with the possibility of significant losses. On the other hand, lower-risk investments offer more stability but typically yield lower returns.

It's essential to assess your risk tolerance before deciding on an investment strategy. If you're just starting out, consider beginning with lower-risk investments, such as bonds or mutual funds, until you become more comfortable with the market. As you gain experience, you may want to consider taking on more risk through individual stocks or real estate.

### The Power of Compounding Interest

One of the most powerful concepts in investing is compounding interest. Compounding is the process by which the value of an investment grows over time as earnings are reinvested to generate additional earnings. In simple terms, it's the idea of earning interest on interest.

### How Compounding Works

Let's say you invest $1,000 in an account that earns 5% annual interest. After one year, your investment will grow by $50, bringing the total to $1,050. In the second year, you'll earn interest on the original $1,000 as well as the $50 in interest from the previous year. The total value of your investment at the end of the second year would be $1,102.50. As time goes on, the amount of interest you earn each year increases, allowing your investment to grow exponentially.

### The Importance of Time

The key to benefiting from compounding is time. The longer you leave your money invested, the greater the impact of compounding. This is why starting to invest early in life can have such a significant impact on your wealth over time.

For example, if you invest $1,000 at the age of 25 and earn a 7% annual return, your investment will grow to around $15,000 by the time you're 65. However, if you wait until you're 40 to make the same investment, you would need to invest over $6,000 to reach the same amount by the time you're 65. Starting early gives your money more time to compound, leading to much larger gains.

**The Rule of 72**

A simple way to estimate how long it will take for your investment to double is the Rule of 72. To use the Rule of 72, divide 72 by your expected annual rate of return. For example, if you expect an 8% return on your investment, divide 72 by 8, which equals 9 years. This means that at an 8% return, your investment will double every 9 years.

The Rule of 72 demonstrates the power of compound interest and highlights the importance of starting your investment journey as soon as possible.

**How to Start Investing with Small Amounts of Money**

One of the most common misconceptions about investing is that you need a large amount of money to get started. In reality, you can begin investing with as little as $50 or $100. Many investment platforms and brokerages offer low or no minimum investment requirements, making it easier than ever to start building wealth, even on a small budget.

**1. Start with Low-Cost Index Funds or ETFs**

If you're just getting started with investing, consider beginning with low-cost index funds or exchange-traded funds (ETFs). These funds provide broad market exposure, which helps diversify your risk while keeping fees low. With as little as $50 or $100, you can purchase shares in an index fund or ETF that tracks the performance of major stock indices like the S&P 500.

Index funds and ETFs allow you to invest in a wide variety of companies without having to pick individual stocks. This diversification reduces risk, which is especially important when you're just starting out and have a smaller investment amount.

### 2. Use a Robo-Advisor

A robo-advisor is an automated investment service that creates and manages a diversified portfolio for you based on your risk tolerance and financial goals. Robo-advisors typically have low fees and low minimum investment requirements, making them an excellent option for beginners with small amounts of money.

By using a robo-advisor, you can invest in a diversified portfolio of stocks, bonds, and other assets without needing to be an expert in investing. These services typically use algorithms to rebalance your portfolio over time and ensure that your investment strategy aligns with your long-term goals.

### 3. Dollar-Cost Averaging

Dollar-cost averaging (DCA) is a strategy that involves investing a fixed amount of money at regular intervals, regardless of market conditions. By investing consistently, you take advantage of both up and down market movements, which helps smooth out the volatility and reduces the impact of short-term market fluctuations.

For example, if you invest $100 every month into an index fund, you'll buy more shares when the market is down and fewer shares when the market is up. Over time, this strategy helps you average out the cost of your investments and reduces the risk of investing a lump sum of money at the wrong time.

### 4. Dividend Investing

Dividend investing is another way to start investing with small amounts of money. Dividend stocks pay regular cash dividends to shareholders, which can be reinvested to purchase more shares. This allows you to take advantage of compounding even with a small initial investment.

Many brokerage firms allow you to reinvest dividends automatically, which means you don't have to do anything to take advantage of compounding growth. Over time, reinvested dividends can significantly increase the value of your investment.

**5. Invest in Real Estate with REITs**

If you're interested in real estate but don't have enough money to buy property, consider investing in Real Estate Investment Trusts (REITs). REITs are companies that own and operate income-producing real estate. By investing in REITs, you can gain exposure to the real estate market without having to buy property yourself. Many REITs have low minimum investment requirements, making them accessible to investors with small amounts of money.

**Conclusion**

Investing is one of the most effective ways to build long-term wealth, and you don't need a lot of money to get started. By understanding the basics of investing, the power of compounding interest, and how to invest with small amounts of money, you can set yourself on the path to financial independence.

The key to successful investing is consistency, patience, and a long-term perspective. While there will be market ups and downs, staying the course and continuing to invest over time will allow you to take full advantage of compounding and grow your wealth. Whether you're just starting with a small amount of money or you're already an experienced investor, remember that every dollar invested today is a step toward achieving your financial goals.

# Chapter 17: The Role of Networking and Relationships in Financial Success

When most people think about building wealth, they often focus on strategies like investing, saving, or managing money. While these elements are crucial to financial success, there's another powerful, often overlooked, force at play: relationships. The power of networking and forming strong, supportive relationships cannot be underestimated. In fact, networking is often the secret ingredient that propels people to achieve significant financial success.

In this chapter, we'll explore how relationships can create wealth opportunities, how to build a network that supports your financial growth, and the importance of mentorship and collaboration. By the end of this chapter, you'll see how cultivating meaningful relationships can serve as a catalyst for not just achieving financial success but sustaining it for the long term.

**How Relationships Can Create Wealth Opportunities**

The role of relationships in creating wealth cannot be overstated. At its core, wealth is not just about money—it's also about access. And relationships provide access in ways that money alone cannot. Building a robust network of contacts and maintaining meaningful relationships with those around you creates opportunities that might not otherwise be available. These opportunities can take many forms: partnerships, business deals, job offers, investment opportunities, and more.

**1. Access to Knowledge and Expertise**

One of the greatest advantages of building strong relationships is the access they provide to knowledge and expertise. When you network with people who have experience in different industries or areas of finance, you can learn valuable insights that help you make better decisions. Whether it's understanding market trends, learning how to evaluate investment opportunities, or getting tips on business management, relationships can provide access to the kind of information that accelerates your financial success.

For instance, if you want to get involved in real estate investing, knowing someone who is already successful in the field can provide you with guidance. They can share their experiences, advise you on potential risks, and introduce you to trusted contractors, brokers, or financial advisors who can help you along the way. Without this network, you might struggle to find the information you need to get started.

**2. Collaborative Opportunities**

Wealth is often built through collaboration, not isolation. The most successful entrepreneurs and investors are those who surround themselves with talented people and leverage their collective strengths. When you collaborate with others, you can pool resources, expertise, and skills to accomplish things that would be difficult, if not impossible, on your own.

For example, an entrepreneur might partner with a financial expert to launch a new product line. By combining the entrepreneur's vision with the financial expert's knowledge of capital raising and financial management, they create a partnership that greatly enhances the chances of success. Similarly, an investor might team up with a skilled developer to start a real estate project, with each party contributing their strengths. These types of collaborations open up doors to wealth-building opportunities that would not be possible if you tried to do everything on your own.

**3. Business and Investment Deals**

Relationships also play a key role in securing lucrative business and investment deals. Many opportunities in the business world are not advertised—they are offered through trusted relationships. Investors often rely on their networks to find exclusive deals, and business owners frequently rely on personal connections to secure funding or strategic partnerships. The more relationships you build with influential and successful people, the more opportunities will present themselves.

For example, many entrepreneurs get their start by finding an investor through a connection in their network. This can lead to the capital they need to launch their business and the guidance they need to succeed. Similarly, investors often receive early access to high-value deals through their relationships with entrepreneurs, business owners, or other investors.

In this sense, wealth creation becomes a team sport. No one achieves financial success entirely on their own. Relationships are often the key to finding and securing the right opportunities at the right time.

**Building a Network That Supports Your Financial Growth**

Now that we've explored how relationships can create wealth opportunities, let's look at how to build a network that supports your financial growth. Developing a strong and supportive network requires a proactive approach, intention, and effort. Here are some strategies for cultivating relationships that will serve your financial goals:

**1. Prioritize Quality Over Quantity**

When it comes to networking, it's not about collecting business cards or having hundreds of LinkedIn connections. The key is to focus on building a few deep, meaningful relationships that can lead to tangible opportunities. It's better to have a small group of highly supportive, trusted individuals who are genuinely interested in helping you succeed than a large group of acquaintances who don't provide much value.

Look for people who share your values, interests, and financial goals. These individuals will be the ones who can offer you the most relevant advice, resources, and support. Invest your time and energy in these relationships, nurturing them over time.

**2. Provide Value to Others**

Networking is a two-way street. It's not just about what you can get from others—it's also about what you can give. When you approach relationships with a mindset of generosity and mutual benefit, you'll be more likely to build strong, lasting connections.

Think about how you can help others in your network. Share valuable resources, introduce them to people who can help them, or offer your expertise when needed. When you give first, you create a sense of goodwill and reciprocity that makes people more willing to help you when the time comes.

**3. Leverage Online Platforms**

In today's digital age, online platforms are a great way to expand your network. LinkedIn, Twitter, and industry-specific forums can connect you with professionals from all over the world. While face-to-face networking is important, online platforms allow you to engage with a broader range of people and find those who share your interests and goals.

When engaging online, focus on being authentic. Share valuable insights, comment thoughtfully on others' posts, and offer your expertise in a way that adds value to the conversation. Over time, you'll build a reputation as a knowledgeable and trustworthy individual, which can attract opportunities and connections.

**4. Attend Industry Events and Conferences**

Another excellent way to build your network is by attending industry events and conferences. These gatherings offer an opportunity to meet like-minded individuals, learn from experts, and engage in meaningful discussions. Whether it's a financial seminar, an entrepreneur's conference, or a real estate networking event, these environments are ripe for making connections that can lead to valuable opportunities.

When attending these events, don't just focus on the people who can directly help you. Be open to connecting with a wide range of people, as you never know where the next opportunity will come from. Build relationships with speakers, fellow attendees, and organizers. Follow up after the event with personalized messages to solidify your connections.

**5. Seek Out Mentorship**

Mentorship is one of the most powerful ways to accelerate your financial growth. A mentor is someone who has already achieved success in an area that you're interested in and is willing to share their knowledge and experiences with you. Having a mentor can provide you with invaluable insights, help you avoid costly mistakes, and provide accountability as you work toward your goals.

To find a mentor, look for someone who resonates with your goals and values. Reach out to them and explain why you admire their work and how you believe they could help you on your journey. Be respectful of their time, and be open to learning from their experiences. A good mentor will challenge you, guide you, and help you see opportunities you might have missed.

**The Importance of Mentorship and Collaboration**

While building a strong network is essential, the true power of relationships lies in mentorship and collaboration. Mentorship provides the guidance and support you need to navigate the complex world of finance, while collaboration amplifies your ability to achieve success. Both elements are crucial to long-term wealth creation.

Mentorship helps you accelerate your growth by providing direct access to the knowledge and experience of someone who has already achieved what you're striving for. A mentor can provide you with practical advice, introduce you to new opportunities, and help you avoid common mistakes. In many cases, mentorship can be the difference between success and failure.

Collaboration, on the other hand, allows you to combine resources and expertise with others to achieve mutual goals. By working together, you can leverage the collective strengths of a group, which increases the likelihood of success. Whether it's starting a business, launching a new product, or investing in real estate, collaboration opens up new possibilities and accelerates wealth-building efforts.

**Conclusion**

Networking and relationships are powerful tools in your wealth-building journey. By cultivating meaningful relationships, offering value to others, and seeking out mentorship and collaboration, you open the door to countless opportunities. Remember, wealth creation isn't just about money—it's about access, knowledge, and the support of those around you. Surround yourself with a network of like-minded individuals who share your financial goals, and you'll find that your path to wealth becomes smoother, faster, and more fulfilling.

# Chapter 18: Managing Setbacks and Staying Focused on Your Financial Goals

Life is full of unexpected challenges, and the journey to financial success is no exception. Whether it's an investment that doesn't pan out, a business venture that falters, or an unforeseen financial emergency, setbacks are part of the process. The key to achieving lasting wealth is not avoiding setbacks but learning how to manage them effectively. The ability to bounce back from financial challenges, maintain focus on your long-term goals, and stay resilient in the face of adversity is what separates the financially successful from those who give up.

In this chapter, we'll explore how to bounce back from financial setbacks, why resilience is critical to building wealth, and how to stay motivated even when the road to financial freedom seems long and uncertain. By the end of this chapter, you'll have a deeper understanding of how setbacks are not obstacles but opportunities to grow, learn, and ultimately achieve your financial goals.

### How to Bounce Back from Financial Setbacks

One of the most important skills to develop on your financial journey is the ability to bounce back from setbacks. A financial setback can take many forms—a job loss, an unexpected expense, a failed investment, or even a personal financial crisis. The disappointment and stress that accompany these events are real, but the way you respond to them can make all the difference.

**1. Acknowledge the Setback Without Letting It Define You**

The first step in bouncing back from a financial setback is to acknowledge the situation without letting it define who you are or your future. It's easy to fall into the trap of self-blame, feeling as if the setback somehow reflects your worth or abilities. But the truth is, setbacks happen to everyone, and they do not define your future potential. Every financially successful person has experienced failures or setbacks. What sets them apart is their ability to bounce back stronger than before.

Take a moment to accept the reality of the situation. Whether it's the loss of a job or an investment that didn't turn out as planned, confronting the setback head-on allows you to move forward without getting stuck in denial or frustration. Once you've acknowledged the setback, you can move on to the next step: assessing the situation.

### 2. Assess the Situation and Learn from It

Financial setbacks often offer valuable lessons if you're willing to learn from them. After a setback, take a step back and assess what went wrong. Was it poor planning? Was it an unrealistic expectation? Did you fail to properly research an investment or business venture? Whatever the reason, it's essential to analyze the situation objectively.

Once you've identified what went wrong, use the experience to inform future decisions. Understanding why something didn't work is crucial to ensuring that you don't make the same mistake again. The process of learning from setbacks is what transforms them from failures into opportunities for growth. Remember, no one achieves success without facing and learning from failures along the way.

### 3. Create an Action Plan for Recovery

After assessing the setback and learning from it, the next step is to create an action plan for recovery. This might involve cutting back on spending, finding additional sources of income, revisiting your investment strategy, or simply giving yourself time to regroup before diving back into your financial goals. The key is to take proactive steps toward regaining your financial footing.

If the setback was related to a financial goal, reframe it within the context of your larger vision. Instead of focusing on the short-term disappointment, focus on what you can do to get back on track. Set new, smaller goals to help you regain momentum and build back your confidence. These incremental wins will help you stay focused on the bigger picture and prevent you from becoming overwhelmed by the magnitude of the setback.

### 4. Take Care of Your Emotional Well-being

Financial setbacks can take a toll on your mental and emotional health. It's easy to become stressed, anxious, or frustrated when things don't go as planned. However, your emotional well-being is just as important as your financial health. Taking the time to manage your emotions during tough times can help you maintain clarity and make better decisions moving forward.

Consider incorporating practices such as mindfulness, journaling, or talking with a supportive friend or mentor to process your emotions and release any negativity. Emotional well-being provides the mental clarity needed to think through solutions and move forward with a renewed sense of purpose.

## The Importance of Resilience in Wealth Building

Resilience is a quality that is often spoken about in the context of personal growth, but it's especially important when it comes to wealth building. Wealth is not something that happens overnight—it's the result of consistent effort, wise decisions, and the ability to overcome challenges along the way.

Resilience is the ability to withstand or recover from difficult situations. In financial terms, it's about being able to weather the ups and downs of life and still stay focused on your goals. Here's why resilience is critical in your wealth-building journey:

### 1. Wealth is Built Over Time

The process of building wealth is a marathon, not a sprint. It requires patience, discipline, and a long-term mindset. Along the way, there will inevitably be setbacks—investments that go wrong, unexpected expenses, or market downturns. Resilience allows you to persevere through these obstacles without giving up on your ultimate goals.

In fact, some of the wealthiest individuals in the world have faced significant setbacks in their careers. For instance, Warren Buffett famously lost money early on in his investing career, but he used those experiences as stepping stones to greater success. Resilience is about staying the course and learning from each setback rather than letting it derail your plans.

### 2. Resilience Fuels Problem-Solving and Innovation

When you encounter a financial setback, resilience helps you think creatively to overcome the challenge. Rather than simply focusing on the problem, resilient individuals look for solutions. This proactive mindset is essential when it comes to wealth building. Resilience encourages you to explore new options, pivot when necessary, and keep working toward your financial goals, even if the path isn't as clear as you'd like it to be.

Resilience also helps you stay calm under pressure, which is crucial for making good decisions. In times of financial hardship, many people panic and make impulsive decisions that can further jeopardize their financial situation. Resilience allows you to pause, assess the situation logically, and find the best way forward.

### 3. Resilience Creates Mental Toughness

Building wealth requires mental toughness—the ability to keep going when things get tough and to stay focused on your long-term objectives, even when immediate results aren't visible. Resilience cultivates mental toughness by teaching you to deal with adversity and stay committed to your vision, no matter how many obstacles arise.

This mental toughness is crucial when you face difficult decisions, such as choosing between taking a loss and holding on to an investment or deciding whether to continue pursuing a business idea that has not yet taken off. Resilient individuals stay focused on the long-term rewards, even when the short-term situation feels discouraging.

**Staying Motivated During Tough Times**

Financial setbacks can take a toll on your motivation. It's easy to become disheartened when things aren't going as planned or when you feel as if you're not making progress toward your financial goals. However, maintaining motivation during tough times is essential to your success. Here's how you can stay motivated, even when the road to financial freedom feels long and difficult:

**1. Revisit Your 'Why'**

When you experience a setback, it's important to reconnect with your deeper motivations. Why did you set your financial goals in the first place? Was it to achieve financial freedom, provide a better life for your family, or create a legacy? Revisit your "why" to remind yourself of the bigger picture. This will reignite your passion and determination to keep moving forward, even when things aren't going your way.

**2. Break Your Goals Into Smaller, Achievable Steps**

One of the reasons people lose motivation during tough times is because they focus too much on the big picture. When the end goal feels too far out of reach, it's easy to feel overwhelmed and lose motivation. To stay motivated, break your larger goals down into smaller, more manageable steps. Focus on what you can achieve today, this week, or this month. Celebrate these small wins, and use them as fuel to keep moving forward.

**3. Surround Yourself with Positive Influences**

The people you surround yourself with can have a significant impact on your motivation. When you're going through a tough time, seek out individuals who can offer support, encouragement, and perspective. This might be a mentor, a trusted friend, or a supportive community. Positive influences can help you stay motivated by reminding you of your potential and offering advice on how to overcome obstacles.

### 4. Maintain a Positive Mindset

A positive mindset is crucial to staying motivated during challenging times. Instead of focusing on what's going wrong, focus on what you can control and what's going right. Use setbacks as learning experiences, and remind yourself that each challenge is an opportunity to grow. A positive mindset helps you stay resilient and motivated, even in the face of adversity.

### Conclusion

Setbacks are inevitable on the path to financial success, but they don't have to define your journey. By developing the ability to bounce back from challenges, cultivating resilience, and staying motivated even in tough times, you'll be able to navigate the ups and downs of wealth building with confidence and determination. Remember that setbacks are not the end—they are opportunities to learn, grow, and ultimately achieve the financial success you desire. Stay focused on your long-term goals, and keep pushing forward, no matter the obstacles in your way.

# Chapter 19: Living a Life of Abundance: Beyond Money

Financial success is often viewed as the key to unlocking the doors to a better life. For many, the pursuit of wealth and financial freedom is the ultimate goal. However, once the basics of financial security are achieved, many individuals find themselves wondering: What's next? How do I create a fulfilling life beyond just accumulating money? The truth is that financial success, while important, is just one aspect of living an abundant life. True abundance encompasses not just money but also personal growth, health, relationships, and a sense of purpose.

In this chapter, we will explore how financial success impacts other areas of life, why giving back and creating value are essential components of an abundant life, and how to achieve a balanced and fulfilling life that goes beyond the pursuit of money. By the end of this chapter, you will understand that true abundance comes from integrating wealth with purpose, relationships, and personal well-being.

**How Financial Success Impacts Other Areas of Life**

While financial success undoubtedly provides comfort, security, and freedom, it also has a ripple effect that can influence other areas of life. The ability to manage money wisely can empower individuals to lead more fulfilling and meaningful lives. Here's how financial success can positively impact various aspects of life:

**1. Personal Freedom and Time**

Financial success gives you the freedom to live life on your terms. When you are not burdened by the constant worry of bills, debt, or paycheck-to-paycheck living, you gain the freedom to prioritize what matters most to you. This freedom can manifest in various ways. You might choose to travel more, spend more time with family, pursue hobbies or passions, or simply enjoy the luxury of time without financial constraints.

Additionally, financial success allows you to make decisions based on your values rather than financial necessity. You may have the ability to leave a job that drains your energy or pursue a career that aligns with your passions. This freedom enables you to live a life that is more in line with your authentic self, free from the shackles of financial pressure.

## 2. Health and Well-Being

It's often said that "money can't buy happiness," but it's important to recognize that financial success can provide the resources to support your health and well-being. Good health is an essential part of living a fulfilling life, and having financial security can make it easier to invest in your physical and mental health.

From affording quality healthcare and healthier food to having the means to hire personal trainers, nutritionists, or mental health professionals, financial success gives you the ability to prioritize your well-being. Moreover, with fewer financial stresses, you are better able to maintain a positive mindset and reduce anxiety, which in turn supports overall mental health.

## 3. Relationships and Social Connections

Money can't buy love, but financial security certainly allows you to foster stronger relationships. When you're not constantly worrying about your finances, you can invest more time and energy in your relationships. You may find that financial success allows you to spend quality time with your partner, children, friends, and family, creating deeper connections and experiences that strengthen those bonds.

Furthermore, financial stability allows you to give to others, whether it's through meaningful gifts, charitable donations, or simply offering support in times of need. Financial success can also open doors to meeting new people who share similar values and interests, expanding your network and creating opportunities for growth and collaboration.

**4. Personal Growth and Education**

Financial success provides the resources to invest in personal development and education. Whether you want to attend workshops, take courses, or read books on topics that interest you, having the financial means to do so allows you to continuously grow as a person. The more you invest in your knowledge and skills, the more you are able to contribute to the world around you.

Additionally, when your basic financial needs are met, you can focus on developing your emotional intelligence, spiritual awareness, and intellectual capabilities. Personal growth is not just about acquiring material wealth, but about cultivating the qualities that make you a better person, partner, and member of society.

**5. Sense of Purpose and Contribution**

Finally, financial success allows you to live a life of purpose. When you achieve a level of financial stability, you no longer have to focus solely on survival or securing your financial future. This shift enables you to think about how you can contribute to the world in a meaningful way. Whether it's by pursuing a passion project, starting a nonprofit, or dedicating your time to causes that matter to you, financial success gives you the freedom to make a difference.

The sense of purpose that comes from creating something larger than yourself can be incredibly fulfilling. It provides you with motivation to continue growing and contributing, which often leads to greater satisfaction and happiness.

**The Importance of Giving Back and Creating Value**

One of the most profound aspects of living an abundant life is the ability to give back and create value for others. While accumulating wealth is important, the true joy of financial success often comes from using your resources to improve the lives of others and make a positive impact on the world.

**1. The Joy of Giving**

There's a deep sense of fulfillment that comes from giving back. Whether it's through charity, volunteering, or simply helping a friend or family member, giving creates a sense of connection and community. Studies have shown that people who regularly give to others experience greater happiness and life satisfaction. Giving not only helps others but also helps you grow as a person.

When you are financially successful, you have the opportunity to make a more significant impact on the lives of others. You can contribute to causes that align with your values, whether that's through financial donations, supporting small businesses, or volunteering your time and expertise. The act of giving is an essential part of creating an abundant life, as it reinforces the idea that wealth is not just for personal enjoyment but for the betterment of the world around you.

**2. Creating Value for Others**

True abundance is about creating value—not just accumulating wealth. When you focus on creating value, whether it's through your business, investments, or personal endeavors, you contribute to the well-being of others. This can take many forms: providing products or services that improve people's lives, sharing your knowledge and expertise with others, or building a community that supports mutual growth.

Creating value is also about leaving a legacy that extends beyond money. When you contribute positively to the lives of others, whether through mentorship, teaching, or charitable work, you create a ripple effect that continues to impact generations to come. This is where true abundance lies—not just in what you have, but in what you give.

### 3. Building a Legacy

As you achieve financial success, it's important to think about the legacy you want to leave behind. A legacy is not just about passing down wealth; it's about passing down values, lessons, and a sense of purpose. Consider how you can leave an impact that lasts long after you're gone.

Building a legacy involves thinking beyond your immediate family or circle and considering how your work, contributions, and resources can benefit future generations. This could mean establishing scholarships, creating an endowment, or supporting charitable foundations. It's about leaving behind a world that is better than the one you found, and ensuring that the values of abundance, generosity, and purpose are carried forward.

### Living a Balanced, Abundant Life

To truly live an abundant life, it's essential to find balance. While financial success is important, it should never be the sole focus of your life. A life of abundance is about integrating wealth with personal well-being, fulfilling relationships, and a sense of purpose. Here are some ways to achieve that balance:

### 1. Prioritize Your Health

Your health is the foundation for all other areas of life. Without good health, financial success and personal growth are meaningless. Prioritize regular exercise, nutritious food, and mental health practices like meditation or therapy. When you take care of your body and mind, you're better equipped to handle the challenges of life and enjoy the fruits of your labor.

### 2. Nurture Your Relationships

No amount of money can replace meaningful relationships. Take the time to invest in your relationships with family, friends, and loved ones. Strong relationships provide emotional support, joy, and a sense of belonging. These connections are just as important, if not more so, than financial success in creating an abundant life.

### 3. Cultivate Gratitude

Gratitude is a powerful tool for creating abundance. By focusing on the blessings you already have, you attract more of what you appreciate. Make it a habit to practice gratitude daily. Whether it's keeping a gratitude journal or simply taking a moment each day to reflect on what you're thankful for, cultivating a sense of gratitude helps you stay grounded and content, regardless of your financial status.

### 4. Stay True to Your Values

Finally, living a balanced life means staying true to your core values. Financial success should never come at the expense of your integrity, your health, or your relationships. Make decisions that align with your values, and remember that the journey to success is just as important as the destination. True abundance is about creating a life that is rich in purpose, connection, and well-being.

### Conclusion

Living a life of abundance goes far beyond the pursuit of money. While financial success provides the foundation for a fulfilling life, it's the integration of wealth with health, relationships, purpose, and contribution that truly creates an abundant life. By focusing on creating value, giving back, and nurturing the things that truly matter, you can live a life that is rich not just in material wealth but in meaning and fulfillment. True abundance is a mindset—a way of being that transcends money and touches every aspect of your life. Embrace it, and you will unlock a life of limitless potential and joy.

# Chapter 20: Creating Your Own Path to Financial Freedom

The pursuit of financial freedom is a deeply personal journey, one that requires dedication, vision, and a willingness to embrace change. Financial freedom is not merely about having enough money to cover your needs, but about having the ability to make choices that align with your values, goals, and dreams. It's about breaking free from the constraints that money can place on your life, and gaining control over your financial future.

In this chapter, we will explore how you can take ownership of your financial journey, set long-term wealth-building strategies, and embrace the power of continuous growth and adaptation. By the end of this chapter, you will understand that financial freedom is a journey that requires not just strategy and planning, but the resilience to keep going, the ability to adapt to changes, and the confidence to carve out your own unique path to success.

**Taking Ownership of Your Financial Journey**

The first step toward achieving financial freedom is taking full ownership of your financial journey. Too often, people find themselves stuck in financial patterns that are driven by external circumstances or societal expectations, rather than their own desires or goals. To break free from this cycle, you must recognize that you are in control of your financial future. You have the power to make choices, shape your destiny, and craft the life you truly want.

Taking ownership begins with understanding where you currently stand. This means assessing your current financial situation with brutal honesty. Take a hard look at your income, expenses, debts, and savings. Understand your spending habits, your financial goals, and where you may be falling short. Don't shy away from the uncomfortable truths. This self-awareness is crucial, as it lays the foundation for change.

Once you have a clear picture of your current financial situation, the next step is to take responsibility for it. This is where you stop blaming external factors, such as the economy, your job, or your upbringing, for your financial circumstances. While external factors may influence your situation, it's important to recognize that you still have the power to change your path. No one else can do it for you. Whether you've made mistakes in the past or are starting from scratch, the key is to take responsibility for your actions moving forward.

Taking ownership also means committing to learning and growing. You don't have to have all the answers right now, but you need the willingness to learn. The world of finance is constantly evolving, and there is always something new to discover. From investment strategies to budgeting techniques, there are countless resources available to help you build your financial knowledge. Take the initiative to read books, listen to podcasts, attend seminars, or consult with financial advisors. The more you learn, the better equipped you will be to make informed decisions.

Ownership of your financial journey also means developing the mindset of a creator. You are not just a passive participant in your financial life—you are an active creator. When you take ownership, you begin to realize that you are the architect of your financial future. This shift in mindset is powerful because it empowers you to make intentional choices, seek opportunities, and create a life that reflects your values and aspirations.

### Setting Long-Term Wealth-Building Strategies

While achieving financial freedom may seem like a distant dream, it is attainable with the right strategies in place. The key to long-term wealth-building is to develop a plan that aligns with your goals and values, and to stick with it over time. This is not about seeking instant gratification or chasing get-rich-quick schemes. True financial freedom is a result of consistent, deliberate actions over time.

### 1. Defining Your Vision of Financial Freedom

The first step in creating a long-term wealth-building strategy is to define what financial freedom means to you. This vision will be the guiding light for all of your decisions. For some, financial freedom may mean retiring early and traveling the world; for others, it might mean achieving the ability to spend more time with family, pursue hobbies, or start a business. Your vision will be unique to you, and it's important to clarify what it looks like so that you can work toward it with purpose.

Take some time to sit down and envision your ideal life. What does financial freedom look like in the context of your values, desires, and aspirations? Write down your vision in detail, and refer to it regularly as a reminder of why you are working so hard toward your financial goals. This vision will serve as both your motivation and your blueprint for success.

### 2. Setting SMART Financial Goals

Once you have a clear vision of your desired financial future, the next step is to set specific, measurable, achievable, relevant, and time-bound (SMART) financial goals. Without clear goals, it can be difficult to stay focused and motivated on your financial journey. Your goals should be broken down into both short-term and long-term objectives.

Start by setting short-term goals that are achievable within the next 1 to 3 years. These might include paying off a certain amount of debt, building an emergency fund, or increasing your income through a side hustle. These short-term goals will give you a sense of progress and help build momentum as you work toward your long-term objectives.

Next, set long-term goals that align with your vision of financial freedom. These might include saving for retirement, buying a home, or building a diverse investment portfolio. Long-term goals require more patience and discipline, but they are essential for creating lasting financial freedom. Break these goals down into smaller milestones so that you can track your progress and make adjustments as needed.

### 3. Building a Diverse Investment Portfolio

Investing is one of the most powerful ways to build long-term wealth. While saving money is important, it's the growth of your money that will lead to financial freedom. To achieve this, you need to develop a diverse investment portfolio that aligns with your risk tolerance, time horizon, and financial goals.

Start by educating yourself on different types of investments, such as stocks, bonds, real estate, and mutual funds. Diversification is key to reducing risk and increasing the potential for returns. A well-balanced portfolio should include a mix of asset classes that work together to achieve your long-term financial goals.

Remember that investing is a marathon, not a sprint. It's important to take a long-term view and avoid making decisions based on short-term market fluctuations. Stay disciplined and consistent, and allow your investments to grow over time. Compound interest is a powerful force that can help accelerate the growth of your wealth if you allow it to work for you.

### 4. Creating Passive Income Streams

One of the hallmarks of financial freedom is the ability to generate passive income—income that comes in without requiring active effort. This could include rental income from real estate, dividends from stocks, royalties from intellectual property, or earnings from a business that runs without your constant involvement.

Building multiple streams of passive income can significantly increase your financial security and speed up the journey to financial freedom. Start by identifying areas where you can create passive income and gradually invest in these opportunities. Over time, the income from these sources will compound and provide you with greater financial independence.

**5. Budgeting and Debt Management**

No wealth-building strategy is complete without an understanding of budgeting and debt management. A well-designed budget allows you to manage your money effectively, ensuring that you are saving and investing enough to meet your goals. Additionally, managing debt is crucial for achieving financial freedom. Pay off high-interest debt first, and avoid accumulating unnecessary debt that could hinder your progress.

Budgeting is not about restricting yourself—it's about making intentional choices with your money. Allocate funds toward savings, investments, and debt repayment, and make sure you are living within your means. The more disciplined you are with your budget, the quicker you will be able to reach your wealth-building goals.

**The Power of Continuous Growth and Adaptation**

The journey to financial freedom is rarely a straight path. Along the way, you will face obstacles, setbacks, and changes in circumstances. The key to long-term success is embracing continuous growth and adaptation. Financial markets, technologies, and opportunities are constantly evolving, and your ability to adapt will determine your success.

**1. The Importance of Learning**

The most successful individuals are those who never stop learning. Financial education should be an ongoing pursuit. Stay informed about changes in the economy, new investment opportunities, and financial strategies. Read books, listen to podcasts, and seek advice from mentors who can help you expand your knowledge and skills.

As you learn, apply what you've learned to your financial journey. Don't just accumulate knowledge—use it to take action. Experiment with different strategies, track your results, and adjust as needed. The more you learn and apply, the better your chances of achieving financial freedom.

**2. Embracing Failure and Resilience**

Failure is a natural part of any journey, and financial freedom is no exception. You will face challenges and setbacks along the way, whether it's a bad investment, an unexpected expense, or a market downturn. The key is to embrace failure as a learning opportunity, rather than a roadblock. Resilience is essential for long-term success. When things go wrong, don't give up—use failure as a stepping stone to success.

**3. Adapting to Change**

The world is constantly changing, and so are your financial circumstances. The ability to adapt is a crucial skill for achieving financial freedom. Whether it's changes in the job market, fluctuations in the stock market, or personal life events, staying flexible and open to new opportunities will help you stay on track toward your goals.

As you move forward, continue to reassess your financial strategies and make adjustments as needed. Remember that your financial journey is dynamic, and it's important to be agile in the face of change. The more adaptable you are, the more resilient you'll be in the pursuit of financial freedom.

**Conclusion**

Creating your own path to financial freedom is a deeply rewarding process that requires ownership, strategy, and continuous growth. By taking responsibility for your financial journey, setting clear goals, and embracing the power of adaptation, you can build a future that aligns with your dreams. Financial freedom is not an overnight achievement, but with dedication and persistence, it is attainable. Keep your vision in focus, stay disciplined, and always be open to learning and growing. Your path to financial freedom is yours to create, and with the right mindset and strategies, you can achieve lasting success and fulfillment.

## Conclusion: Your Journey to Wealth Begins Now

As you close the pages of this book, it's important to reflect on the powerful principles of money mindset mastery that you've discovered. What you've learned is not just about accumulating wealth, but about shaping your thoughts, behaviors, and habits to attract the financial success you desire. Achieving true financial freedom is not a destination—it's a journey that begins with your mindset, and it's a path that requires dedication, resilience, and a commitment to continuous growth.

### Summing Up the Core Concepts of Money Mindset Mastery

Throughout this book, you've explored a multitude of concepts that, when combined, form the foundation of a wealthy mindset. The journey to financial abundance starts with understanding the power of your thoughts. As you've seen, your mindset influences every financial decision you make, from how you manage your money to how you approach challenges and setbacks. By replacing limiting beliefs with empowering thoughts, you unlock your potential to achieve financial success.

A crucial concept in this book was the understanding that financial freedom isn't just about numbers—it's about mastering your psychology and creating a mindset that aligns with your goals. You've learned how to develop a mindset of abundance, transforming your relationship with money. You've also discovered practical strategies for managing debt, creating passive income, and investing wisely, all of which are essential for long-term wealth creation.

Additionally, the importance of setting clear financial goals and staying disciplined in your approach cannot be overstated. The path to financial freedom requires both strategy and patience. It's about building a sustainable future, not chasing short-term wins. Whether it's through investing, budgeting, or cultivating healthy money habits, each step you take is part of a larger, fulfilling journey toward wealth.

By mastering these core concepts of money mindset mastery, you have laid the groundwork for lasting change. You are now equipped with the tools to not only build wealth but to cultivate the right mindset to sustain it for years to come.

**Final Tips for Staying on Track**

As you embark on your financial journey, remember that progress takes time. The road to wealth and abundance is not always linear, and there will be moments when things feel uncertain. However, by staying consistent and committed to your principles, you will create the financial life you envision. Here are a few final tips to keep you on track:

**1. Stay Committed to Your Goals:** Review your financial goals regularly to ensure you are staying focused. Celebrate small victories along the way, but never lose sight of the larger vision. Keep reminding yourself of the reasons why you are on this journey and what financial freedom means to you.

**2. Keep Learning:** The financial world is constantly evolving. Make it a habit to continue educating yourself about new strategies, investment opportunities, and market trends. Financial literacy is an ongoing process, and the more you learn, the better equipped you will be to navigate challenges and make informed decisions.

**3. Practice Resilience:** You will face setbacks along the way—whether it's an unexpected expense, market volatility, or moments of doubt. Embrace these challenges as opportunities to grow. Resilience is what will help you bounce back stronger and more determined to keep moving forward.

**4. Build a Support System:** Surround yourself with people who encourage your financial growth. Seek out mentors, peers, or online communities who share similar goals and values. A strong support system can offer valuable advice, emotional support, and motivation when you need it most.

**5. Stay Disciplined:** Financial freedom requires discipline. You may encounter temptations along the way to indulge in impulse spending or veer off course, but staying disciplined is the key to building long-term wealth. Stick to your budget, consistently save, and remain focused on your financial goals.

**6. Embrace Change:** Your journey will not be static, and neither will the world around you. Be adaptable and open to new opportunities. As you evolve, so will your financial strategies. Embrace change with confidence, knowing that it's a natural part of the growth process.

### Encouragement for Your Journey Toward Abundance

As you continue your journey toward financial freedom, remember that wealth-building is a marathon, not a sprint. It's a process that requires consistency, patience, and a positive mindset. But it is also an incredibly empowering journey that can lead to greater fulfillment, both financially and personally.

By mastering your money mindset, you've taken the first step in creating a life of abundance and freedom. The strategies and tools shared in this book are powerful, but they are only effective if you take action. Every step you take brings you closer to your goals, and every obstacle you face is a chance to strengthen your resolve and grow.

Believe in your ability to create the life you desire. You are the architect of your financial future, and with each choice you make, you are building the path to your dreams. Your journey to wealth begins now—and the possibilities are limitless.

Stay focused, stay committed, and above all, trust the process. Financial freedom is not a matter of luck—it's a result of deliberate action, the right mindset, and unwavering persistence. You have everything you need to succeed.

Remember: the journey may be long, but the rewards are worth it. Embrace your power, continue learning, and take bold steps forward. Your wealth-building journey is just beginning, and it's filled with endless opportunities to create the life you've always imagined.

## MAXWELL RYDER

Here's to your success—your journey to financial freedom starts today.

www.ingramcontent.com/pod-product-compliance
Lightning Source LLC
Chambersburg PA
CBHW071057240526
45471CB00016B/1984